When God Breathes

Breathes

The smell of God's breath is undeniable

WAYNE KNIFFEN

WESTBOW
PRESS®
A DIVISION OF THOMAS NELSON
& ZONDERVAN

WestBow Press books may be ordered through booksellers or by contacting:

WestBow Press
A Division of Thomas Nelson & Zondervan
1663 Liberty Drive
Bloomington, IN 47403
www.westbowpress.com
844-714-3454

Scripture quotations marked TPT are from The Passion Translation®.
Copyright © 2017, 2018, 2020 by Passion & Fire Ministries, Inc. Used
by permission. All rights reserved. ThePassionTranslation.com.

Scriptures marked (NLT) are taken from the Holy Bible, New Living Translation,
copyright © 1996, 2004, 2015 by Tyndale House Foundation. Used by permission of
Tyndale House Publishers Inc., Carol Stream, Illinois 60188. All rights reserved.

Scripture quotations marked (NKJV) are taken from the New King James Version.
Copyright © 1982 by Thomas Nelson, Inc. Used by permission. All rights reserved.

ISBN: 979-8-3850-2141-3 (sc)
ISBN: 979-8-3850-2142-0 (hc)
ISBN: 979-8-3850-2143-7 (e)

Library of Congress Control Number: 2024905321

Print information available on the last page.

WestBow Press rev. date: 03/15/2024

To every hungry soul desperately seeking to have a deeper intimacy with our heavenly Father and to smell the aroma of His sweet presence.

CONTENTS

Contents

PROLOGUE

"God has transmitted his very substance into every Scripture, for it is God-breathed. It will empower you by its instruction and correction, giving you the strength to take the right direction and lead you deeper into the path of godliness. Then you will be God's servant, fully mature and perfectly prepared to fulfill any assignment God gives you" (2 Timothy 3:16 TPT).

The Passion Translation of 2 Timothy 3:16 is the switch the Holy Spirit used to turn on my desire to write this book *When God Breathes*. I am well aware that to some this title makes it sound like there may be times when God does not breathe. On the contrary, God is breath. Without the breath of God, there would be no life. If God doesn't breathe out, we don't breathe in. Not only does the breath of God impart life, His breath is the only thing that can sustain life. If He stops breathing, we cease to exist.

God brought all of creation into existence by His breath—His spoken word, "Light be" (Genesis 1:3 NKJV). There is something profoundly significant in this verse that is worth paying attention to. God never recalled the light that He released with His breath. Light was never told to stop, to return, or to cease. God told light to be, and it has been expanding ever since at the rate of 186,000 miles per second—in all directions. Can you imagine how far light has traveled since God breathed it into existence? Only God has the answer.

When God formed the physical body from the dust of the

ground for humanity to live in, it was lifeless. "And the Lord God formed man of the dust of the ground" (Genesis 2:7 NKJV). The physical body was created vacant. It was only an "earth house" for the spirit and soul to live in. The body in and of itself cannot know God, love God, or serve God. It was formed with no life residing within. But it had incredible potential, as does all of God's creation. What the human body lacked was the breath of God living on the inside of it. "[And the Lord God] breathed into his nostrils the breath of life; and man became a living being" (Genesis 2:7 NKJV). When God breathes, things come alive. When God breathed the breath of life into Adam, he became a living soul, a speaking spirit. Now he has the ability to know God, love God, and serve God. What made this possible? God imparted His divine nature into Adam when He breathed the breath of life into him. The breath of God is what brings things into existence, and it is God's breath that keeps things from coming apart. Without Him, there is no life, and life can't be sustained without His breath.

There is a wonderful verse in the book of Romans that I quote to myself on a regular basis. It has ministered to me and kept me going when everything seemed to be falling apart more times than I can remember. "*The Spirit of God, who raised Jesus from the dead, lives in you*. And just as God raised Christ Jesus from the dead, *he will give life to your mortal bodies by this same Spirit living within you*" (Romans 8:11 NLT, emphasis added). Process what this verse is saying. As a child of God, the same spirit that raised Jesus from the dead lives inside of you. The God who said, "Light be" (Genesis 1:3) has taken up permanent residence within you. And he made you a promise that he will never leave or forsake you (Hebrews 13:5). Simon Peter echoes this same incredible truth when he said that we are partakers of God's divine nature (2 Peter 1:4). Without the life of God living in us, we have no lives.

As you continue reading *When God Breathes*, I pray you will experience the Lord's presence like never before and that you begin to smell the sweet fragrance of His breath.

ONE

The Written Word Is the Breath of the Living Word

God has transmitted his very substance into every Scripture, for it is God-breathed. It will empower you by its instruction and correction, giving you the strength to take the right direction and lead you deeper into the path of godliness. Then you will be God's servant, fully mature and perfectly prepared to fulfill any assignment God gives you.
—2 TIMOTHY 3:16 (TPT)

The Bible is not simply a book that tells us about God; it is the very breath of God. Paul told Timothy that God transmitted His very substance, His essential nature into every scripture. That makes the written Word the breath of the Living Word. We can read it knowing that we are not only feasting on the bread of life, but we are also smelling the very breath of God. The smell is intoxicating, and it will create a craving deep within us for more of this living bread.

The Word Became Human

As you read this passage in 2 Timothy 3:16 (TPT), keep John 1:1–5, 1:14 (NLT) and the first two chapters of Genesis on the front burners of your mind. It will help you to better understand how God could transmit His very essence, His essential nature, into the scriptures.

> In the beginning the Word already existed. *The Word was with God, and the Word was God.* He (the Word) existed in the beginning with God. God created everything through Him, and nothing was created except through him. The Word gave life to everything that was created, and *his life brought light to everyone.* The light shines in the darkness, and the darkness can never extinguish it. ... So *the Word became human* and made his home among us. He was full of unfailing love and faithfulness. And we have seen his glory, the glory of the Father's one and only Son. (John 1:1–5, 1:14 NLT, emphasis added)

There is a bright flashing red light in this passage that should cause every reader to stop and pay attention to what has been said. "The Word became human" (John 1:14 NLT). This is what makes the written Word the breath of God.

John makes two incredible declarations about the Word. The Word was God, and at the same time, the Word was the second person of the Trinity, the Son of God. The Word was with God, and the Word was God. This is the *us* we read about in Genesis 1: "Then God said, 'Let Us make man in Our own image, according to Our likeness'" (Genesis 1:26 NLT). To whom was God talking? Have you ever wondered? There was no one else present when God began time. We are left with only one conclusion; God was talking to Himself. The story only gets better.

The appointed time came when the Word became human and made His home in the midst of humanity. In other words, God wrapped Himself up in human flesh and birthed Himself in the person of Jesus. Jesus was the very essence of the Father. This is why Jesus answered Philip the way He did, "Lord, show us the Father, and we will be satisfied" (John 14:8 NLT). Jesus said to Philip, "Anyone who has seen me has seen the Father" (John 14:9 NLT). God is now living among His creation in the person of Jesus, who is called the Word. This is the reason He is called Jesus Christ. Jesus addresses His humanity, and Christ reveals His divinity—Immanuel: God is with us. The union of the divine and human natures of Christ in one hypostasis.

Can you imagine being present in that Bethlehem stable the night Jesus was born? As you stare inside that makeshift cradle where Mary laid her baby, you are looking into a manger that is filled with God. The Living Word had become human, making it possible for God to be among humanity in physical form. God literally wrapped Himself up in an earth suit and went through the natural birthing process to bring the heavenly realm into the earthly realm. The thing that separated His birth from the rest of humanity was His conception (Luke 1:26–38 NKJV). Over the years, I've had people ask me to explain this miracle of how the Word became human. I will have to confess it does impress me a little that someone would think I'm smart enough to explain the virgin birth. But that is not going to happen because it is impossible to explain. I would be leery of anyone who said they could. This is why it is called a miracle! If it could be explained, it would not be a miracle; a miracle is inexplicable. If it were possible for someone to explain a miracle, you would not be able to understand it; a miracle is incomprehensible. No one is capable of understanding this incredible event—the Incarnation. It must be received by faith. But there is one thing we can know and should know: Jesus is the very breath of God. This is what motivated John to write, "Whoever denies the Son does not have the Father either; he who acknowledges the Son has the Father also" (1 John 2:23 NKJV). The Word (Jesus) was with God, and the Word (Jesus) was God.

Jesus's first cry came from a stable in Bethlehem at His birth. His purpose for being on the earth had begun. The Word had become human. His last cry came from a cross in Jerusalem at His death. His purpose for becoming human had been completed.

Preparation for the First Christmas

Over the years, I have spent an incalculable amount of time in the first five chapters of Genesis. I have read them, taught them, and written extensively about them. It would not be an exaggeration to say that these five chapters are on my favorite scripture list, for in them we find the law of first mention. I'll give you an example. If you want to know how the human race began, you will find the answer in Genesis. "So God created man in His own image; in the image of God He created him; male and female He created them" (Genesis 1:27 NKJV). This is the first time male and female are mentioned in the scriptures—hence, the law of first mention.

If you are curious about how sin infiltrated the human race, all you need to do is read Genesis 3 (NKJV). This part of the creation narrative had me a little confused for a long time and, I might say, a tad frustrated. I just could not understand why God would allow the enemy to sully His greatest creation—humankind. It was certainly not because He did not have the ability or authority to do so. The question I mumbled under my breath was *Why didn't God step in and do something about it?* Humanity was on the brink of being destroyed, and God did not come to their defense. He knew that the serpent was Satan in disguise, yet it appears He just stood by and allowed the seduction to happen unchallenged. Then again, maybe God did intervene.

God has gifted every person with free will. He will not usurp the rights of an individual to make their own choices. Maybe this is why God did not come to their rescue. This is a great answer, and it's absolutely true that God will not override our free will, but it did not satisfy my inquisitive spirit. Why did God allow the enemy to spoil the apple of His eye by not stepping in when the devil was luring them into disobedience? This question awakened deep within me every time I read Genesis 3. One day while reading chapter 2, the answer to my question jumped off the page and landed in my spiritual inbox. God did step in! Not only did He step in, but He also took care of the problem before there was ever a problem. In Genesis 2, the Creator did intervene before there was ever a need for Him to. You may be thinking right now, *I never knew that*. Satan would say the same thing. He didn't know either.

God's intervention took place when He made a woman in Genesis 2. Let me help you connect some dots before we move on. This will be invaluable later on for us to understand how God is always one step ahead of whatever happens in life. After all, before God starts anything, He finishes it first (Isaiah 46:9–10 NKJV). Think about the young lady God created in Luke 1. Her name was Mary. She experienced a heavenly visitation from the angel Gabriel with a message from her Creator. "And behold, you will conceive in your womb and bring forth a Son, and shall call His name Jesus" (Luke 1:31 NKJV). Mary was a virgin, so how in the world could she have a baby? She was overwhelmed by Gabriel's announcement. This was the reason for her asking, "How can this be, since I do not know a man?" (Luke 1:34 NKJV). Bless her heart, she was as perplexed by this news as I was when I read Genesis 3, causing me to wonder why God did not step in and rescue Adam and Eve from Satan's ruse to convince them that disobeying God, by eating from the forbidden tree, was no big deal. He could have at least cleared His voice.

The birth narrative that we find in Matthew's and Luke's Gospels has its roots in Genesis 2. "So the Lord God caused the man to fall into a deep sleep. While the man slept the Lord God took out one of the man's ribs and closed up the opening. Then the Lord God made a woman from the rib, and he brought her to the man. 'At last!' the man exclaimed 'This one is bone from my bone and flesh from my flesh! She will be called 'woman,' because she was taken from 'man''' (Genesis 2:21–23 NLT). Once again, we see the law of first mention. This is the first mention of prime rib, just saying.

We can choose to look at the creation of humankind from one of three perspectives. We can view the creation of humankind through the lens of God's Word (which I strongly suggest) through the eyes of a man, or we can see it through the eyes of a woman. Ladies first: "God made man, then looked at him and said, 'I can do better than that. I will make a woman.'" Here's a man's perspective: "God made man and rested. Then He created the woman; neither God nor man has rested ever since." Just for the record, the last two perspectives are not biblically accurate, so I strongly suggest that you don't use this information when you share the Christmas story in your Bible study group.

Sometimes the Word of God uses the word humankind to reference the entire human race—to describe human beings collectively (Genesis 1:27 NKJV). Let's stretch the parameters of our thinking for a moment. If we are willing to think outside of the box, it will open up some incredible truths about how God prepared for the first Christmas long before we read the birth narrative of Jesus recorded by Matthew and Luke. God wrapped the first Christmas gift in the book of Genesis.

When we use the term human beings, we are talking about the entire species Homo sapiens, which includes a man, a woman, or a child. As we just said, humankind is often used in the Bible to address the subject of humanity in its entirety. There are many scriptures that speak specifically about humankind. Here is an example: "I am the Lord, *the God of all the peoples* (flesh, humankind) of the world" (Jeremiah 32:27 NLT, emphasis added). The word man is traditionally used to refer to male and female. It also draws a contrast between human beings and animals.

God breathed life into the first man (Adam), and the first woman (Eve). They became living beings (speaking spirits) by the breath of God. "This is the written account of the descendants of Adam. When God created *human beings*, he made them to be like himself. *He created them male and female,* and he blessed them and called them 'human'" (Genesis 5:1–2 NLT, emphasis added). All of creation was given life by the breath of God.

God created Eve physiologically different from Adam for a reason. This difference is what made her the perfect match for him. Adam was the perfect match for Eve as well. And I might add, long before she ever knew she had a need for a soul-mate. By creating physical differences between a male and a female, God was making sure they could fulfill the assignment He had given them; and that was to be fruitful and multiply (Genesis 1:28 NKJV).

The term woman was given to Eve by Adam because she was taken out of him (Genesis 2:21–23 NLT). Even though Eve was a part of humankind, God created her with a womb. Having a womb gave her the ability to do what a man could not do and still cannot do or will ever do. She could conceive and carry a child. This is one of the many anatomical differences that distinguishes a male from a female. But they are both a part of humankind.

Why did God create a wombed helpmate for Adam? As we just referenced, it gave Adam and Eve the ability to fulfill the command given to them. They were told to rule and reign over the earthly realm where God had strategically placed them, in the same way He rules the heavenly realm (Genesis 1:28 NKJV). They were to fill the earth with humankind and to provide governance over all that God had created. Could it be that God knew what would take place in Genesis 3? If He did (I'm convinced He did), then He actually stepped in before there was a need for Him to intervene. Satan was defeated before he seduced Adam and Eve to disobey God in the garden. And his ultimate defeat would come through the womb of a woman. Preparation to restore fallen humankind took place before humankind needed to be restored. Are you beginning to connect the dots?

God was multitasking when He created the woman. He made sure she was the perfect fit for Adam, physically, emotionally, and spiritually. But there was something else God had in mind when He created Adam's perfect fit. He was creating the vehicle that He would use to bring Himself into the earthly realm when the right moment presented itself (Galatians 4:4 NKJV). God made sure Eve was the perfect model in every way.

When God created the first woman with a womb, He was preparing the way for Himself to be the first Christmas gift. "For here is the way God loved the world—*he gave his only, unique Son as a gift*. So now everyone who believes in him will never perish but experience everlasting life" (John 3:16 TPT, emphasis added). This gift was and still remains the best gift that has ever been given to humankind. This gift was addressed to *whosoever*.

When God Breathes Life Begins

There is a heated debate today over when life begins. When is a fetus considered to be a human being? God settled that argument at the beginning of time before there was ever a debate. "You saw who you created me to be before I became me! Before I'd ever seen the light of day, the number of days you planned for me were already recorded in your book" (Psalm 139:16 TPT). God says that life begins at conception. Because His word is true, there will never be a need for Him to change his mind. Truth will always be the truth no matter who may say otherwise.

Human opinions are constantly in a state of flux. It doesn't matter what a university biology professor may say about when life begins, or what a court of law may legislate, or what anyone says; the opinion of humankind means absolutely nothing when it is in competition with the Word of God. The Word of God emphatically declares that life begins at fertilization with the embryo's conception. If you want your mind stretched even further, process this: God knew you before you were conceived. "I knew you before I formed you in your mother's womb. Before you were born I set you apart and appointed you as my prophet to the nations" (Jeremiah 1:5 NLT). I believe it would be wise for us to listen to and agree with the one who knows the answer to a problem before there is ever a problem. Maybe this is our problem; we're listening to the wrong voices. Here is one undeniable fact that you may want to mull over. Those who are in favor of aborting the unborn share one thing in common. They have already been born. I find that disgusting to the nth degree. The debate over when life begins is closed as far as I'm concerned. Life begins the moment God breathes.

Here is an interesting tidbit that I find fascinating. Unmanipulated science also emphatically declares that human life begins at the time of conception. The moment when fertilization takes place, the child's genetic makeup is already complete. Its gender has already been determined, along with its height, hair, eyes, and skin color. The only thing the embryo needs is the time to grow and develop.

From a Garden to a Stable

The written word makes it possible for us to span millenniums of time by simply turning a few pages in our bibles. We can go from the Garden of Eden to a stable in Bethlehem with just a lick of our fingers to that special moment when God kissed the earth with His physical presence. One of the benefits of being able to do this allows us to see why God created the first woman with a womb at the beginning of time. The Word became human (John 1:14 NLT). God is now present in the midst of humanity in the person of His Son, Jesus Christ. What travel arrangements did God use to get here? It was through the womb of a woman. This was His plan long before there was ever a garden. Now we know that God did intervene in Genesis 3 when Satan was scamming Adam and Eve out of their true identities. God stepped in big time, and I might add, at the right time!

The Word that was with God, and the Word that was God, is now living in the midst of humanity (John 1:1–2 NKJV). This is called the incarnation, the union of divinity with humanity in Jesus Christ. Here is another way to say it: Jesus was God in human form. "So the Word became human and made his home among us" (John 1:14 NLT). Jesus was the Child that was born (His humanity), and Christ is the Son (His divinity) that was sent (Isaiah 9:6 NKJV).

God knew what was coming before it ever came. He knew Adam and Eve would capitulate to the seducing spirit that would lead to their removal from the garden. Since He is the all-knowing, all-powerful, and all-present God, He saw the empty manger that was in the stable in Bethlehem long before it ever existed. He reserved it for Himself. This is mind-blowing, to say the least. Meditate on this for a moment. God made a way for humanity to return to Him before humanity ever left Him. He did this by creating a woman with a womb and then breathed life into her. You read that right. God solved the problem of sin before sin ever entered humankind. Remember what God says through Isaiah, before He starts something, He finishes it first (Isaiah 46:9–10 NKJV). He establishes the end from the beginning.

Not only did God see the empty manger in Bethlehem when He began time, but He also saw the cross before time began. "And all the people who belong to this world worshiped the beast. They are the ones whose names were not written in the Book of Life that belongs *to the Lamb who was slaughtered before the world was made* (Revelation 13:8 NLT, emphasis added). Mull this over; there are people who think they can go toe-to-toe with God. If you want to give it a try, go for it. You will be given a new name if you do—victim.

The Written Word Is Our Daily Bread

"For the word of God is *living* and *powerful*, and *sharper* than any two-edged sword, *piercing* even to the division of soul and spirit, and of joints and marrow, and is a *discerner* of the thoughts and intents of the heart" (Hebrews 4:12 NKJV, emphasis added). The written Word of God is filled with life because God transmitted His very substance (essence) into every scripture, for it is God-breathed (2 Timothy 3:16 TPT). And just think, God gave us His written Word so we could hear His heart and be filled with His sweet-smelling presence.

"And there is no creature hidden from *His sight*, but all things are naked and open to *the eyes of Him* to whom we must give account" (Hebrews 4:13 NKJV, emphasis added). There is an obvious shift in this verse from the written word to the Living Word. This is the purpose of the written word; to bring us face-to-face with the Living Word. The more we know God's Word, the better we will know him.

The Word of God was given to be our daily bread, not some fancy dessert we order at a five-star restaurant on special occasions: Like Christmas and Easter. If we have been faithfully eating the Word of God on a daily basis, the people we come in contact with will be able to smell it on our breaths. The smell of the Word of God on our lips cannot be hidden from our friends or from our foes. Let's faithfully gorge ourselves on the word daily. Good table manners are not required either. Roll up your sleeves and dive in; and remember, the written word is the very breath of God.

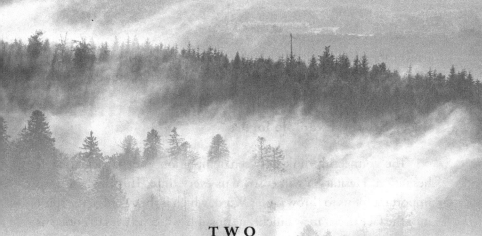

TWO

The Power of God's Breath

Then the man of lawlessness will be revealed, but the
Lord Jesus will kill him with the breath of his mouth
and destroy him by the splendor of his coming.
—2 THESSALONIANS 2:8 (NLT)

Not only does the breath of God have the power to start
time, but His breath has the power to end time as we know
it. When God said, "Light be," light started being and has
been expanding ever since (Genesis 1:3 NKJV). An appointed time
is coming when the Word breathes again. His breath will bring
an end to this world that has been corrupted by humanity's sinful
disobedience (Revelation 19:11–16 NLT). The power of God's breath
is incomprehensible.

The kingdom of darkness has not heard the voice of the Lord for
the last time. That moment will certainly come, and it will be at a
time no one suspects. Jesus's death, burial, and resurrection annulled
the devil's authority but not his power. But the only power he has is
what we give to him, knowingly or unknowingly. The day is coming
when he will be rendered powerless too. His power will be totally,

irrevocably disannulled by the breath of God (2 Thessalonians 2:8 NLT). God will always have the first and last say about everything.

Jesus Set the Example for Us

The connecting link between temptation and participation is hesitation. Hesitation will ensnare us every time. This is why it is so important for us to throw God's Word, which is the sword of the spirit into the face of Satan as quickly as possible when he tries to entice us to act in ways that are not compatible with our new creation natures. The longer we hesitate, the easier it becomes for us to take a bite of the devil's bait. Temptation (the bait) is not a sin, but participation (the bite) is. Hesitation is what enhances our chances to capitulate to the wiles of the devil. We will always overcome temptation when our first response is to declare the written Word of God. My counsel is to quote the word out loud. Not only does the enemy hear the Word of God spoken (which is his kryptonite), but our inner spirits hear it as well. This helps to fortify our resolve to live as victors, not as victims. When we allow the breath of God to breathe through our breaths, we are serving Satan a cease-and-desist order. He must comply.

The first thing Jesus did when He began His public ministry was to demonstrate to us how to overcome temptation and how not to allow temptation to ensnare us. Jesus, called by Paul as the last Adam (1 Corinthians 15:45 NLT), was victorious when the first Adam failed. Satan came fishing in Genesis 3 with only three baits in his tackle box. That was all he needed. His goal was to pluck the apples of God's eyes from the tree of life—humankind. He continues to use the same three baits today because they were and are still very effective in getting people hooked. These three baits are identified for us in 1 John 2:16 (NKJV). They are the lust of the flesh, the lust of the eyes, and the pride of life. Keep this in mind as you continue reading. The bait that Satan uses is not the problem. It is the bite. It doesn't make any difference what bait the tempter uses. If we don't bite, we will never be caught.

How did Jesus deal with temptation? How was He able to do what the first Adam should have and could have done but did not do? The baits Satan used to catch the first Adam in Genesis 3 to get him to disobey God's Word are the same baits he used in his attempt to get the last Adam to disobey God. Unlike the first Adam, Jesus did not take a bite of Satan's bait. Matthew gives us an account of this incredible event. Matthew 4 is Genesis revisited.

John the Baptist was known as the wilderness preacher. His message was simple, and it was anointed by the power and authority of heaven. "Repent of your sins and turn to God, for the Kingdom of Heaven is near" (Matthew 3:2 NLT). John's message on repenting of sins and turning to God was a timely word, for the king of heaven was near. As a matter of fact, He was much closer than John realized.

Jesus departed from Galilee and made His way to the banks of the Jordan River where John was baptizing those who had listened to his message, repented of their sins, and turned to God. When Jesus came and presented Himself to be baptized, John was taken aback on his heels. Can you imagine Jesus asking you to baptize him? Me neither! It is understandable why John responded the way he did. "But John tried to talk Him out of it. '*I am the one who needs to be baptized by you*,' he said, '*so why are you coming to me?*'" (Matthew 3:13–14 NLT, emphasis added) "But Jesus said, 'It should be done, for we must carry out all that God requires,' so John agreed to baptize him" (Matthew 3:15 NLT).

"After his baptism, as Jesus came up out of the water, the heavens were opened and he saw the Spirit of God descending like a dove and settling on him. And *a voice from heaven* said, 'This is my dearly loved Son, who brings me great joy" (Matthew 3:16–17 NLT, emphasis added). When John raised Jesus up from the waters of the Jordan, God spoke from heaven and validated Jesus's identity as His Son. I would love to have seen the faces of those who were present that day. I'm sure the crowd was abuzz with chatter. Things are always stirred when God breathes.

There was someone else present that day. Even though they were hidden and could not be seen by the people, God's breath exposed their presence. This one recognized the voice of God because they had heard it many times before. The smell of God's breath was something they were familiar with as well. This sneaky snake hiding in the shadows is exposed in Matthew 4.

"Then Jesus was led by the Spirit into the wilderness to be tempted by *the devil*. For forty days and forty nights he fasted and became very hungry" (Matthew 4:1–2 NLT, emphasis added). After Jesus was baptized, the spirit of God led Him into the wilderness where He was tempted by the same one who had tempted Adam in Genesis 3, the most cunning of all beasts, Lucifer disguised as a serpent.

For forty days and forty nights, Jesus ate nothing. Matthew's account of this event says that Jesus became very hungry. Now, we know why the tempter began with the lust of the flesh first. This is the most effective bait in Satan's tackle box: The same bait he used when he caught Adam and Eve in Genesis 3. "So when the woman saw that *the tree was good for food*" (Genesis 3:6 NLT, emphasis added). The number one gate that sin usually enters is through the lust of the flesh. The first thing that caught Eve's attention was that the forbidden tree was good for food. The bait of lust is designed to get us to focus our attention on the desires of the flesh even when we know that it is outside the parameters of God's will. This is why it is imperative for us to keep the lust gate closed. When Satan rings the doorbell to lust for the flesh, tell Jesus it is for Him. Let Him answer the door.

When the tempter saw that Jesus was hungry, he tried to seize the moment by opening the flesh gate. It worked on the first Adam, so why won't it work on the last Adam? "If You are the Son of God, command that these stones become bread" (Matthew 4:3 NKJV). First of all, the devil knew Jesus was the Son of God. He was the one that the crowd did not see at the banks of the Jordan River that day when John baptized Jesus. He recognized the voice of God when He spoke from heaven at that baptismal service. He knows how the breath of God smells, and he knows who Jesus is. At one time, he led the angel choirs of heaven in worshipping the one and only true God.

The second thing we need to pay attention to is how the tempter used Jesus's physical need in an attempt to get Him to take the bait, which would open the lust of the flesh gate, giving temptation an entrance into his life. The tempter said to a hungry Jesus, "You are hungry, and here are some stones. Since you are the Son of God, you have the power to turn them into bread. Go for it." Jesus was not going to allow his physical need to control his life. What did Jesus do? He could have cleared His throat, and that would have been enough to put the tempter on the run. Instead he quoted the written Word of God—out loud. When Jesus, the Living Word, took His stand on the written word, He was demonstrating for us how to keep the gate of lust closed. "But He answered and said, 'It is written, Man shall not live by bread alone, but by every word that proceeds from the mouth of God'" (Matthew 4:4 NKJV). Because God has transmitted His very essence into His Word when we take our stand on the written word, we are literally blowing the breath of God in the face of the tempter, which he has no defense against.

Since the tempter was unsuccessful in getting Jesus to open the flesh gate, he switches to the eye gate—the lust of the eyes. The bait of flesh did not catch anything, so maybe the lust of the eye bait will. It certainly worked on humanity at the beginning of time. "When the woman saw that the tree was good for food, that *it was pleasant to the eyes*" (Genesis 3:6 NKJV, emphasis added). Not only did Eve see that the fruit from the forbidden tree would be good to eat, but it was also pleasant to the eyes. The tempter is trying to get Jesus to open the lust of the eye gate, so he can get a toehold.

"Then the devil took Him up into the holy city, set Him on the pinnacle of the temple, and said to Him, 'If you are the Son of God, throw yourself down. For it is written: He shall give His angels charge over you, and, In their hands they shall bear you up, Lest you dash your foot against a stone" (Matthew 4:5–6 NKJV).

What a spectacular event that would be to witness, Jesus jumping off the temple wall in Jerusalem and then a host of angels swooping in to snatch Him up before He touches the stone walkway below. If that were to happen, everyone would believe that Jesus was the Son of God. After all, isn't that why Jesus came to this earth?

Let me call your attention to something that I think is very interesting. It is easy to get so engrossed in what is taking place between Satan and Jesus, that we don't see it. The tempter had the audacity to quote the written word to the Living Word. "For it is written," he said, and he quoted a portion of the Psalm 91. The words "to keep you in all your ways" were cunningly omitted (Psalm 91:11 NKJV). In his letter to the Ephesian church, Paul told them that the Word of God is the sword of the spirit (Ephesians 6:17 NKJV). When Jesus rebuffed the tempter with the written Word of God, He was using the sword of the spirit, and the devil had no defense against it. The written word was cutting him into pieces. In a feeble attempt to stay in the fight, the tempter tried to use the sword of the spirit on Jesus. This was not a wise decision. Jesus parried the tempter's thrust by speaking the truth of the word. "Jesus said to him, 'It is written once again, You shall not tempt the Lord your God'" (Matthew 4:7 NKJV).

The Word of God calls Satan a liar and identifies him as the father of all lies. He does not have the ability to tell the truth (John 8:44 NKJV). What the tempter will do is speak half-truth as if it were the whole truth; this makes it a lie. Jesus did not fall for his half-truth. How Jesus responded to this temptation is the way we need to respond when the tempter comes to us fishing, trying to get us to open the gate of the lust of the eyes. By quoting the written word we are using the sword of the spirit. The tempter has absolutely no defense against it.

Even though Satan was taking a shellacking, he did not give up yet. He had one more bait in his tackle box. The bait was called the pride of life. This last bait was what led to the crunch that affected the entire human race. Eve wanted the wisdom that she thought eating the fruit would give her. It is never wise to do what God says for us not to do. The third gate was opened—the pride of life. The Bible says that Eve took some of the fruit and ate it. Then she gave some to Adam, and he ate it too. Adam and Eve swallowed the bait of Satan, hook, line, and sinker. Their fall affected us all. All three doors had been opened: the door of lust of the flesh, the door of lust of the eyes, and the door of pride. Their hesitation between temptation and participation had cost them dearly, and I might add, it cost all of humanity too.

This is the purpose for the last Adam coming into the earthly realm. He came to buy back what humanity had sold in the beginning—their souls. It wasn't to jump off of the roofs of buildings to demonstrate who he was; it wasn't to turn stones into bread; but it was to live a sinless life, die a sinner's death, and conquer death and the grave for those who will put their faith and trust in Him. Jesus was lifted up on a cross so the world could see who He was. There would be no angels swooping down to deliver Him even though they would have had they been dispatched. Jesus died alone. Pontius Pilot could not kill Him, Satan could not seduce Him, and the grave could not hold Him. He is still the Living Word, the very breath of God.

"Next the devil took him to the peak of a very high mountain and showed him all the kingdoms of the world and their glory. 'I will give it all to you,' he said, '*if you will kneel down and worship me*'" (Matthew 4:8–9 NLT, emphasis added). Satan comes out in the open and shows his hand. He wants to be worshipped. When we hesitate between temptation and participation, we will find ourselves doing just that—worshipping the tempter.

Don't forget that in Matthew 4 Jesus is setting the example for us on how not to be overcome by temptation, whether it be lust of the flesh, lust of the eyes, or the pride of life. We overcome the enemy of our souls by keeping our focus on the Living Word, and by using the written word as the sword of the spirit. A lie can never stand in the presence of truth for very long. When we follow Jesus's example, we win.

"Jesus said to him, 'Away with you, Satan! For it is written, 'You shall worship the Lord your God, and Him only you shall serve'" (Matthew 4:10 NKJV). Jesus did not carry on a conversation with the devil. He did not try and debate him. All He had to do was breathe the written word in his face.

Can you believe the devil had the unmitigated gall to try and seduce the Son of God? He had millennia of practice to perfect his skills. He had been quite successful in seducing men and women into taking his baits. But he underestimated his targeted victim this time. He was trying to ambush the one who had created him. Jesus did not fall for the tempter's ruse. He kept the doors closed so that the lust of the flesh, the lust of the eye, and the pride of life had no access when the tempter came knocking. Jesus took His stand on the solid foundation of the Word of God. What Jesus did, we can do. If we abide in His word, which is truth, the truth we know will not only set us free, but the truth will keep us free. Jesus demonstrated to us how we can overcome the enemy of our souls no matter how he may disguise himself or what bait he chooses to fish with.

It does not matter what door the devil knocks on to see if he can gain entrance into our lives. We will be triumphant over temptation every time when we follow the example Jesus set for us. Jesus was the Living Word, and He took His stand on the written word, which was the breath of God. This is our example of victorious living. We can keep standing when those around us are falling if our faith is deeply planted in Jesus Christ. We will never have to fear the wind. There is power in the breath of God.

"Then the devil left Him, and behold angels came and ministered to Him" (Matthew 4:11 NKJV). The devil walked away with his tail tucked between his legs, and angels came and took care of Jesus.

Why did the devil walk away? It was because he had no more arrows in his quiver. He ran out of ammo. The only things he has in his arsenal to lure us away from the Lord are the lust of the flesh, the lust of the eyes, and the pride of life. This is so important for us to understand. You and I will never be tempted by anything new.

This is why Paul wrote these words to the church in Corinth, "*The temptations in your life are no different from what others experience. And God is faithful.* He will not allow the temptation to be more than you can stand. When you are tempted, he will show you a way out so that you can endure" (1 Corinthians 10:13 NLT, emphasis added). This is good news! We will never be used as a test case for the enemy to try out a new temptation. The temptations that the deceiver used to lure the first man away from God's presence in Genesis 3 are the same weapons he will use on us.

Satan knows that if he can be successful in limiting your time in the written word, it will lessen the chances of you limiting him by the word. The devil is keenly aware that the written word is the breath of God. God's breath is breathing through us when we quote the written word.

File this away in your memory bank so you can easily retrieve it: Temptation is everywhere, but so is our God. Satan uses temptation to weaken us. God uses temptation to strengthen us. Overcoming or being overcome by temptation becomes our choice.

Submit to God—Resist the Devil

Temptation doesn't become a sin until you agree with it. Jesus was tempted in every way as we are, but He never once gave in. "So then, we have a great High Priest who has entered heaven, *Jesus the Son of God*, let us hold firmly to what we believe. This High Priest of ours understands our weaknesses, *for he faced all the same testings we do, yet he did not sin.* So let us come boldly to the throne of our gracious God. There we will receive his mercy, and we will find grace to help us when we need it most" (Hebrew 4:14–16 NLT, emphasis added).

So how do we escape when we find ourselves being challenged to choose between fidelity and infidelity? We look to Jesus as our example. He faced every temptation that we will ever face, but He never gave the enemy access by opening any gates. He never took a bite of the devil's baits. No matter how attractive sin may be, we need to see it the way God does. How does God see sin? God sees sin as a thief that comes to steal, kill, and destroy. He knows sin will keep His children from enjoying their birthright privileges as new creations. He sees sin as being destructive, worthless, putrid, disgusting, and nasty. God hates sin because it is the very antithesis of His nature, and I might add that sin is also the antithesis of our new creation's nature as well.

Assured victory over sin comes from our submitting and resisting. "Therefore, *submit to God. Resist the devil* and he will flee from you" (James 4:7 NKJV, emphasis added). It is imperative that we keep James 4:7 in the right order. We are told to submit and then resist. Resisting without submitting is a recipe for defeat. It is true that resisting the devil is a part of this verse. However, if resisting is our beginning point, we will find ourselves on the short end of the stick most of the time because we will be relying on our own strength. Sometimes we may win a skirmish or two, but most of the time, we will get pummeled. By submitting to God first, we have the full backing of our heavenly Father when we resist the devil. Listen to the words of David: "Praise the Lord, *who is my rock*. He trains my hands for war and gives my fingers skill for battle. *He is my loving ally and my fortress, my tower of safety, my rescuer. He is my shield*, and *I take refuge in him*. He makes the nations submit to me" (Psalm 144:1–2 NLT, emphasis added). If the truth of these two verses ever becomes a living reality in your life, it just may leave you spoiling for a fight.

The Written Word Is the Breath of God

Satan is well aware that the written word is the power of God's breath. This is why he will do whatever it takes to keep you from spending time in the word. He knows God's word is truth and that it will not only set you free, but the Word of God also has the power to keep you free. "Jesus said to those Jews who believed Him, *"If you abide in My word*, you are My disciples indeed. *And you shall know the truth*, and *the truth shall make you free"'* (John 8:31–32 NKJV, emphasis added). Look closely at what Jesus said. Truth doesn't set you free. Truth is truth whether you are free or not. The written word declares that it is the truth you know that makes you free. Let God breathe His breath through you so you are empowered to submit to God and resist the enemy.

THREE

The Holy Spirit Is the Breath of God

So Jesus said to them again, "Peace to you! As the Father has sent
Me, I also send you." And when He had said this, He breathed
on them, and said to them, "Receive the Holy Spirit."
—JOHN 20:22 (NKJV)

It was a sad day—Jesus had died—Hearts that had been overflowing with hope were now filled with sadness. Joseph of Arimathea, along with Nicodemus, took the body of Jesus, bound it with strips of linen cloth and spices, and then placed the body in a tomb that had never been used before in the garden where he had been crucified. Buried with Jesus that day were the hopes and dreams of those who loved and followed him.

Early on Sunday morning while it was still dark, Mary Magdalene slowly made her way to the place where they had laid the body of Jesus. Her spirit was heavy, and her eyes were filled with tears as she approached the tomb. I cannot imagine the thoughts that must have been invading her mind or the pain she felt in her soul. What? To her utter amazement, she noticed that the stone had been rolled away from the entrance of the tomb. Instead of looking inside, she ran to find Peter and John to tell them the stone had been rolled away from the mouth of the tomb. When she found them, she said, "They have taken the Lord's body out of the tomb, and we don't know where they have put him" (John 20:2 NLT). Without hesitating, Peter and John took off for the grave site as fast as they could run.

John outran Peter, so he was the first to arrive at the unsealed tomb. He immediately stooped down and looked inside. He saw the grave clothes but no body. When Simon Peter arrived, he went straight inside the empty tomb. He too saw what John had seen. The grave clothes were there but no corpse. "Then the disciple who had reached the tomb first *(John)* also went in, and he saw and believed—for until then they still hadn't understood the Scriptures that Jesus must rise from the dead. Then they went home" (John 20:8–10 NLT, emphasis added).

Mary made her way back to the tomb. She was weeping uncontrollably. When she stooped down to peep inside, she saw two white-robed angels. One was sitting at the head, and the other one at the foot of the place where the body of Jesus had been lying. The angels asked Mary why she was crying: "'Because they have taken away my Lord,' she replied, 'and I don't know where they have put him'" (John 20:13 NLT).

Clouded by an emotional fog, Mary turned away from the entrance of the tomb. She saw the figure of a man standing close by. Her immediate thought was *It's the gardener.* In her confused state of mind, she did not recognize it was Jesus. "'Dear woman, why are you crying?' Jesus asked her. 'Who are you looking for?'" (John 20:15 NLT). Thinking it was the gardener talking to her, she answered, "'Sir,' she said, 'if you have taken him away, tell me where you have put him, and I will go and get him'" (John 20:15 NLT).

Mary's life was about to be radically transformed when Jesus called her name, "Mary!" As soon as Jesus spoke her name, she knew who it was. "She turned to him and cried out, 'Rabboni!' [Hebrew for teacher]. 'Don't cling to me,' Jesus said 'for I haven't yet ascended to the Father. But go find my brothers and tell them, I am ascending to my Father and your Father, to my God, and your God'" (John 20:16–17 NLT). Filled with resurrection hope, Mary went and found the disciples and told them she had seen the Lord. He is alive!

On the evening of resurrection Sunday, the disciples were meeting behind locked doors. They were afraid they might be hunted down and put to death by the Jewish leaders. After all, they had killed Jesus. Suddenly Jesus was standing in the same room with them. Can you imagine what that moment was like? The doors were shut and locked, and just like that, Jesus was standing in their midst. No wonder he said, "*Peace* be with you" (John 20:19 NLT, emphasis added). The stone that had sealed the entrance of the tomb was not rolled away to let Jesus out. It was removed to allow us to see inside. If a grave could not hold him, what was a locked door to the Lord?

The first thing Jesus did after saying, "Peace be with you" was to show His disciples the wounds in His hands and His side. They were amazed and filled with joy when they saw the Lord. Pay close attention to what Jesus said and did next. "Again he said, 'Peace be with you.' Then *he breathed on them* and said, '*Receive the Holy Spirit*'" (John 20:21–22 NLT, emphasis added). Read that verse again, slowly this time. The risen Lord told His disciples to receive the Holy Spirit when He breathed on them. This was the beginning of something He would finish in the second chapter of the book of Acts.

Holy Spirit's Identity

The Holy Spirit is not a thing as many may think. He is not an influence or a power. The Holy Spirit is the presence of Christ living on the inside of everyone who has accepted and received Jesus as their Lord and Savior. The moment we had our born-from-above experience with Jesus Christ, the Holy Spirit moved in and took up permanent residence. Every child of God has the very breath of the

Creator living inside them. He made a promise that He would never leave or forsake those who belonged to Him (Hebrews 13:5). There would never be a time when He would pack His bags and move out. The Holy Spirit is also called the comforter, advocate, helper, counselor, intercessor, and strengthener. Jesus called Him the spirit of truth (John 14:17 NLT).

In John 14–16, Jesus is having a straightforward talk with His disciples about His impending death, resurrection, and ascension. He told them that the day was drawing near, but He did not want them to be discouraged. That was not something they wanted to hear. To add to their bewilderment, Jesus told them that it would be to their advantage when He did leave. "'But now I go away to Him [God the Father] who sent Me, and none of you asks Me, where are you going? But because I have said these things to you, sorrow has filled your heart. Nevertheless I tell you the truth. *It is to your advantage that I go away; for if I do not go away, the Helper* [Holy Spirit] *will not come to you*'" (John 16:5–7 NKJV, emphasis added). To complete His atonement for sin, it would be necessary for Jesus to leave the earthly realm and return to the Father (John 12:31–32 NLT). If Jesus had remained on earth in person, then the object of the disciples' faith (and ours) would always be focused on a tangible external person. This would limit our dependence on Christ. When He was physically present, we would be good to go. But when He was not physically present, who would we turn to? What would we do if we did not have the Holy Spirit living inside of us? Having the abiding presence of the Holy Spirit in us is what makes it possible for every child of God to have invariable, intimate, immediate, indwelling contact with God. Instead of relying on someone *outside* ourselves, as believers in Christ, we can focus on the voice of God on the *inside* of our innermost being. The breath of God is the Holy Spirit. We need to learn how to discern His voice in the midst of all the chaotic worldly chatter going on around us. We need to be so in tune with God, that when He breathes, we are able to recognize the smell of His breath. I assure you the enemy of our souls does.

The breath of God (Holy Spirit) provides every believer with a constant personal indwelling union with God. So having the Holy Spirit residing in us is to our advantage. He is the breath of God that saves us, He is the breath of God that sustains us, and He is the breath of God that satisfies us.

The Promise of Another Helper

"If you love Me, keep my commandments. And I will pray the Father, and He will give you *another* Helper, that He may abide with you forever—*the Spirit of truth*, whom the world cannot receive, because it neither sees Him nor knows Him; *but you know Him, for He dwells with you and will be in you*. I will not leave you orphans; I will come to you" (John 14:15–18 NKJV, emphasis added). There are two words for another in the Greek language. One is heteros which means another of a different kind. The other word is allos which means another of the same kind. The *another* Jesus used in this passage means another of the same kind. In other words, the Holy Spirit is the same as Jesus. The Holy Spirit is the breath of Christ living inside us. As we said earlier, the Holy Spirit is our comforter, advocate, helper, counselor, and intercessor. He is the spirit of truth.

"Jesus replied, 'All who love me will do what I say. My Father will love them and *we will come and make our home with each of them*. Anyone who doesn't love me will not obey me. And remember, my words are not my own. What I am telling you is from the Father who sent me. I am telling you these things now while I am still with you. But *when the Father sends the Advocate as my representative—that is, the Holy Spirit*—he will teach you everything and will remind you of everything I have told you'" (John 14:23–26 NKJV, emphasis added). Did you notice that Jesus addressed the Holy Spirit as *He*? You cannot separate the Father from the Son or the Son from Holy Spirit. It is also impossible to separate the Son from the Father or Holy Spirit from the Son. The Father, the Son, and the Holy Spirit are one and the same. The Holy Spirit living inside us is God living His life through us.

The Wind of the Spirit

Under the cover of darkness, Nicodemus, a Jewish religious leader and a Pharisee, came to speak to Jesus. He began the conversation like this, "'Rabbi,' he said, 'we all know that God has sent you to teach us. Your miraculous signs are evidence that God is with you'" (John 3:1 NLT). Jesus's response knocked Nicodemus out of his sandals. "Jesus replied, 'I tell you the truth, unless you are born again, you cannot see the Kingdom of God'" (John 3:3 NLT). Nicodemus's thoughts were focused on the natural realm. How is it possible for a grown man to go back into his mother's womb and be born a second time? That does not make sense. Nicodemus's mindset was on physical birth while Jesus was focused on spiritual birth. "Jesus replied, 'I assure you, no one can enter the Kingdom of God without being born of water and the spirit. Humans can only reproduce human life (water), but the Holy Spirit gives birth to spiritual life (spirit). So don't be surprised when I say, 'You must be born again.' *The wind blows wherever it wants. Just as you can hear the wind but can't tell where it comes from or where it is going, so you can't explain how people are born of the Spirit'"* (John 3:5–8 NLT, emphasis added).

Jesus revealed to Nicodemus that to be born again means you must be born from above. Natural life comes by being born from below, and spiritual life comes by being born from above. It is possible to explain the natural birth process to a great degree, but it is impossible to explain spiritual birth. It is inexplicable because being born from above is a miracle, and miracles cannot be explained. If you could, they would not be miracles.

Jesus used the wind to illustrate to Nicodemus how the spirit of God operated. You can hear the wind, feel the wind, and you can see the effects of the wind. But it is impossible to see the wind or to know where it comes from or where it is going. If you find that hard to believe, the next time you feel the wind, try to catch a handful of it. It is not possible to see the wind with our physical eyes.

In like manner, you cannot see the Holy Spirit any more than you can see the wind. It is impossible to see the Holy Spirit come and go. But you can hear the voice of the Holy Spirit, see the presence of the Holy Spirit, see the results of the Holy Spirit, and feel the power of the Holy Spirit. According to Jesus, the wind blows wherever it wants, and so does the Holy Spirit.

In Acts 2:1–4, we see Jesus completing what he started in John 20:22 when He breathed on His disciples and told them to receive the Holy Spirit. "On the day of Pentecost all the believers were meeting together in one place. *Suddenly, there was a sound from heaven like the roaring of a mighty windstorm*, and it filled the house where they were sitting. Then, what looked like flames or tongues of fire appeared and settled on each of them. *And everyone present was filled with the Holy Spirit* and began speaking in other languages, as the Holy Spirit gave them this ability" (Acts 2:1–2 NLT, emphasis added). This is the promise Jesus made to those who had placed their trust and confidence in him. "Do not leave Jerusalem until *the Father sends* you *the gift* he promised, as I told you before. John baptized with water, but in just a few days *you will be baptized with the Holy Spirit.* (Acts 1:4–5 NLT, emphasis added). On the day of Pentecost, Jesus fulfilled His promise of the Father, sending the gift of His Spirit to permanently indwell His children.

The Creating and Sustaining Breath of God

The Word of God is unequivocal about how creation came into being. "*By the word of the Lord* the heavens were made. And all the host of them *by the breath of His mouth*" (Psalm 33:6 NKJV, emphasis added). The Lord simply breathed everything into existence. The same breath that brought everything out of the unseen realm into the seen realm was breathed into the first man Adam. That is the moment he became a living soul, a speaking spirit. Without the breath of God, there is no life. Let me say something that I've already said twice: If God doesn't breathe out, we don't breathe in. The same breath that God breathed into the first man, resides in you too if you are a child of God. That is a mind-blowing revelation. The spoken Word of God that brought order out of disorder, light out of darkness, lives in us. When God breathes, things happen.

The writer of the book of Hebrews echoes Psalm 33:6. "*By faith* we understand that *the worlds were framed by the word of God*, so that the things which are seen were not made of things which are visible" (Hebrews 11:3 NKJV, emphasis added). One translation says that everything God created is sustained by His word. What this verse in Hebrews says is amazing, to say the least. If things were not made from things that can be seen, then everything that can be seen was made out of things that cannot be seen. That means the things that cannot be seen are more real than the things that can be seen. The unseen spiritual world is more real than the seen physical world. It's no wonder this verse begins with *by faith* we understand this.

The breath that creates life is the same breath that sustains life. "The Son radiates God's own glory and expresses the very character of God, and *he sustains everything* by the mighty power of his command [word, breath]" (Hebrews 1:6 NLT, emphasis added). Not only does the breath of God have creating power, but it also has sustaining power.

The name Holy Spirit encapsulates both the spirit's power and divine purpose. The same word is used for wind and spirit in both the Greek of the New Testament (*pneuma*) and the Hebrew of the Old Testament (*ruach*). This is why we can say with confidence and clarity that the Holy Spirit is the very breath of God.

In Genesis 1, we see the breath (ruach) of God bringing into existence all of creation. "In the beginning God created the heavens and the earth. The earth was formless and empty, and darkness covered the deep waters. *And the Spirit of God was hovering* over the surface of the waters" (Genesis 1:1–2 NLT, emphasis added). The word hovering describes a mother hen brooding over her clutch of eggs so they will hatch. This may help us to picture in our minds what was taking place at the very beginning of the beginning. The Spirit of God was hovering, brooding over a formless, empty, and dark earth. Then God breathes—"Let there be light, and there was light" (Genesis 1:3 NLT).

The only thing it took for God to bring light into existence was for Him to breathe. The wind of His breath has creative power. Not only does the breath of God create, but His breath also sustains what He creates. The moment God told light to be, it started existing, traveling in all directions at the speed of 186,000 miles per second. Have you noticed that God never told light to stop existing or come back? Light has existed since God breathed it into existence. It is impossible for the finite human mind to even begin to grasp how far light has traveled since God brought it forth by His breath. And just think, if we could somehow get out in front of the light as it continues to expand, we would hear the voice of God, "Light be." Light is sustained by the same breath that released it.

After God had set everything in motion through the wind of His voice, He created humanity. "And the Lord God formed man of the dust of the ground, *and breathed into his nostrils the breath of life; and man became a living being*" (Genesis 2:7 NKJV, emphasis added). This is when human life began. The Hebrew word for form is *yi'ser*. It is a word that is used to describe the skills of a potter, a sculptor, or an artist. A potter or sculptor does not create something from nothing. They are gifted with the ability to bring into existence something that already has substance like clay, a piece of marble, or stone. God took the dirt He had already created (existing substance) and formed the body of the first man. Before we move on, let's slow down a little so we can see the difference between the physical and spiritual. After God had formed the body of humankind out of dirt, what was that body able to do? The answer is—not one thing. The physical body was formed by God with no life inside of it. Therefore, the body cannot know God, love God, or serve God. The physical body is just a shell, an earth suit for humankind to live in while on this earth.

Since God is the source of all life, He is the only one who could put life into the body He had formed. How did He do it? "[God] breathed into his nostrils the breath of life, and man became a living being" (Genesis 2:7 NKJV). It was the breath of God that imparted life into this lump of dirt. When God breathed into the nostrils of Adam who had been formed from the dust of the ground, Adam became a talking spirit, a living soul. Without the breath of God, it would be impossible for humanity to exist. Like we said in the prologue if God doesn't breathe out, we don't breathe in. The breath (spirit) of God living on the inside of us is what confirms our identities as spiritual beings. We are not physical beings who have spirits; we are spiritual beings living in physical bodies. This is a game changer in the way we live our lives if this truth ever gets hold of us.

We Carry God's Breath Inside Us

Some years ago, a British film was made to tell the story of a man from Calcutta. He had moved to London seeking to fulfill his dreams of making a fortune. He was not in London long when he saw a lady get hit by a bus. When he ran to her crippled body to see what he could do to help her, he noticed she was not breathing. Quickly he applied mouth-to-mouth resuscitation. His quick response revived this injured lady. When this woman had the opportunity to meet and thank this gentleman who had saved her life, he told her, "Madam, my life is now in you."

The Word of God says that before we accepted and received Jesus Christ as our Lord and Savior, we were dead in our trespasses and sins. Borrowing from our story about the lady who got hit by a bus in London, it could be said this way: We had been hit by a sin bus. *"And you* He made alive, *who were dead* in trespasses and sins" (Ephesians 2:1 NKJV, emphasis added). When God breathes on us as He did the first man Adam, His life comes into us. His breath is the only thing that can give life. Our heavenly Father breathes on us, in us, and then through us.

There is an old hymn written by B. B. McKinney that I love. The title of it is "Holy Spirit, Breathe on Me." The chorus of the hymn says it all.

> Breathe on me, breathe on me,
> Holy Spirit, breathe on me;
> Take now my heart, cleanse every part,
> Holy Spirit, breathe on me.

"The grass withers and the flowers fade, but the word [breath] of God stands forever" (Isaiah 40:10 NLT, emphasis added). This scripture is amazing. God is eternal, which means He has no beginning or end; therefore, His breath is not limited by time or eternity.

The heart of the Father is to breathe on us, in us, and then through us. The next time you take a breath, remember that when God breathes out, you can breathe in.

FOUR

God's Breath Lives in You

> Have you forgotten that your body [God's house] is now the
> sacred temple of the Spirit of Holiness, who lives in you? You
> don't belong to yourself any longer, for the gift of God, the Holy
> Spirit [God's breath], lives inside your sanctuary [body].
> —1 CORINTHIANS 6:19–20 (TPT, EMPHASIS ADDED)

When you had your born-from-above experience with Christ, God, in the person of the Holy Spirit moved in and took up permanent residence, you are now God's house. Think about what our lives would be like if we really understood that God lives on the inside of us. That's right. The God who spoke all things into existence lives in you. The God who performed and still performs miracles has chosen you as His home. The God who raised Jesus from the grave has made you His sacred temple. Wherever we go and whatever we may be doing, we are carrying the breath of God on the inside of us. If we ever get a revelation of this truth, the way we live our daily lives will be radically different. As believers, we are the houses of God.

Paul's Warning to the Church in Corinth

When there is a schism in the ranks of the fellowship of believers, it's because they have shifted their focus and the main thing is no longer the main thing. In his first letter to the church in Corinth, Paul addressed their divisive and immature behavior. Even though they had been children of God for an extended period of time, they were still nursing on milk when they should have been feasting on solid food. This immaturity was expressed through their character and conduct. There was great division among them over personalities. One group was enamored with Paul, and Apollos was the favorite of others. This had caused a rift in their fellowship. They had taken their eyes off of Jesus and were focused on human flesh, on personalities. This cliquish mentality is still prevalent in the body of Christ today. It is so easy for us to get hung up on what preachers/teachers we like best. To keep us from falling into this trap, we must stay on our spiritual toes. We must never allow personalities no matter how polished and shiny they may be, to usurp control of our allegiance to Christ.

To correct their behavior, Paul reminds them that he and Apollos had different assignments, but they had the same purpose. They were both servants of the Lord. "After all, who is Apollos? Who is Paul? We are only God's servants through whom you believed the Good News. *Each of us did the work the Lord gave us. I planted the seed* in your hearts, and *Apollos water it, but it was God who made it grow.* It's not important who does the planting, or who does the watering. *What's important is knowing that it is God who makes the seed grow*" (1 Corinthians 3:5–7 NLT, emphasis added). We can plant, we can water, but only God can make the seed grow. Because this is true, we must keep God in the crosshairs of our focus. Without Him, there would never be a harvest. We need to keep planting and watering and then trust God to mature the seed. God receives all the glory when we do this. And He should.

Building God's House

Paul uses two illustrations in 1 Corinthians 3 to illustrate what being the house of God looks like. The first one is from agriculture—"You are God's field." The second one is from architecture—"You are God's building." We are God's field, and we are God's building. Let's focus our attention on being God's house. For a house to be structurally sound, it must have a solid foundation to rest upon. If we fudge on laying a good foundation, it's just a matter of time when the house falls down. It's not if it falls, it's when it falls. A weak foundation will cause structural damage to the entire house.

Paul is not talking about a physical house when he says, "You are God's building." He is talking about our personal lives as believers, individually and corporately. Our foundation is Christ. "For no one can lay any foundation other than the one we already have—Christ Jesus" (1 Corinthians 3:11 NLT). Christ is the only sure foundation a person can build one's life on that will last for time and eternity. Once the proper foundation has been laid, building the house can commence.

There are two sources of building materials that we have at our disposal. One comes from the devil's lumber yard, which is wood, hay, and straw. These building materials are perishables, and on the day of judgment, fire will test the quality. There's only one thing wood, hay, and straw can do when exposed to fire—burn. The other source for building materials comes from God's treasure house. They are gold, silver, and jewels. Unlike wood, hay, and stubble, these building materials are permanent. They will not burn when tested by fire. Every person has a choice of which materials they will use when building their lives on a sure foundation. Some think, *Why use gold when wood will do? Why use silver when hay will do? Why use jewels when straw will do?* There is an appointed day coming called the day of judgment when fire reveals if a person's work has any value. "But on the judgement day, fire will reveal what kind of work each builder has done. The fire will show if a person's work has any value. If the work survives, that builder will receive a reward. But if the work is burned up, the builder will suffer a great loss. The builder will be saved, but like someone barely escaping through a wall of flames" (1 Corinthians 3:13–15 NLT). That illustration Paul uses is quite graphic, and it is imperative that we listen to what he says. This letter was not only addressed to the Corinthian church (in late AD 56 or early AD 57), but it is for the church today.

Paul used the analogy of building a house to illustrate how important it is for us to make wise choices when it comes to growing and maturing in our spiritual lives individually and collectively. Cheap substitutes are just that—cheap. Inferior building materials may not cost as much as the best materials, and they may give the appearance of being adequate, but there will come a day when these building materials will be tested by the fire. Wood, hay, and stubble will be consumed.

Conversely a wise builder with integrity will use only the best materials—gold, silver, and jewels. These are the permanent building materials that come from God's treasure house. Since we are God's house, His holy temple, why wouldn't we want to use the best materials available?

Back in the seventies and eighties, there was an oil filter commercial with a slogan that became very popular—"You can pay me now or pay me later." In other words, you can pay a little more for a good oil filter now or you can pay much more later when your car breaks down. This slogan was soon used as a catchphrase of comparison for just about everything. Something you need may cost you more now, but if you put it off because of the expense, you will pay much more later.

Maybe this would be a good slogan to sum up 1 Corinthians 3:11–14. Why use expensive gold, silver, and jewels when we can use wood, hay, and straw? We sure could save a lot of time and money. That is certainly true. But we should not forget that there is an appointed day coming when the quality of our work will be tested by fire, not the quantity of our work.

Pay Now or Pay Later

The story is told of a young man who wanted to follow in the footsteps of his dad. His heart's desire was to become an architect and join his father's architectural firm. His dreams came true. After graduating from college, he went to work for his dad as an apprentice. This young man was incredibly gifted and talented. The day finally arrived when his dreams came true. He was given the assignment and responsibility to design and oversee the firm's next custom home build. It was this young man's time to rise and shine. The chance for him to demonstrate to his father his design and construction abilities had finally come. Whatever he does with this project will have his father's name and reputation endorsing it. He was determined to make good on the trust his father had invested in him.

This young architect's dad was known for his integrity, honesty, and unsullied character. He would only use the best construction materials on all of his projects. His word was his bond even if it cost him personally. He always gave his clients his best. Cutting corners or using inferior building materials were never on his radar screen. He never settled for inferior building materials for his construction projects. If any mistakes were ever made on one of his home builds, he would not hide it or pass the extra cost for rectifying it on to his clients.

After completing the blueprints of his first assignment, this young man began to entertain the thought, *If I were to cut back on how much concrete is used on the foundation and most of the other construction materials, I could save a bundle which would mean more money in my pocket, and for my dad's firm.* No one would really know. After all, the exterior covering would hide any compromised interior flaws. This was the choice he made. He certainly did not exemplify the character qualities of his father or the sterling reputation of his dad's architecture firm.

The construction began. For the next ninety days, this young man provided oversight for his first home construction project.

Things were looking good. The foundation did not have the thickness that was required for structure stability, inferior materials were used, and many corners were cut to save a dollar. Everything was going as planned. The day came when the job was completed. It was tour day. He and his father drove to the construction site to inspect his first build. As they drove to the site, their conversation was about this young man's upcoming wedding. He was marrying his high school sweetheart. His dad was telling him how proud he was of him for completing his first home build and for being the kind of man his future bride could trust and rely on.

When they drove into the driveway, his father was impressed with what he saw. Before they got out of their vehicle, the young man said, "Dad, thank you for trusting me to build my first home. I will always remember this in a special way. But there's one thing that you've never told me. Who is this home for?" His father smiled as he handed him the keys to this home and said, "Son, this home is for you and your future bride—congratulations." This young man and his bride would live in a home that was built with wood, hay, and straw. He had chosen to use inferior building materials, beginning with the foundation. Instead of paying now, he paid later. Choices have consequences, so choose wisely.

This is in essence what Paul was saying to the church at Corinth. You have the right foundation under you, so be wise concerning the materials you use in building your lives on this foundation. Taking shortcuts and using inferior materials like wood, hay, and straw will be very costly later on. "Don't you realize that all of you together are the temple of God and that *the Spirit of God lives in you*? God will destroy anyone who destroys this temple. For *God's temple is holy, and you are that temple*" (1 Corinthians 3:16–17 NLT, emphasis added). If God's temple is you and if God's temple is holy, what does that make you? It is time for us to start living out what we have living within—the breath of God.

The Breath of God Is a Person

If you were given the assignment to introduce the Holy Spirit, how would you do it? How can we adequately introduce someone who we really don't know that well? Most of the time when you hear someone talking about the Holy Spirit, they will use the word *it* as if the Holy Spirit were a thing, a mysterious power, a source, or an influence. The Holy Spirit is a person, and this person lives inside of you. God's breath in you is the Holy Spirit (John 20:22).

How to resolve this issue about the Holy Spirit's identity is simple. Our answer is found in John's Gospel. Pay attention to how Jesus introduced the Holy Spirit. "[Jesus] But I will send you the *Advocate*—the *Spirit of truth. He* will come to you from the Father and will testify all about me" (John 15:26 NLT, emphasis added). Jesus would not identify the Holy Spirit as He if He were an *it*. After all, Jesus should know. The Holy Spirit is the very breath of God living on the inside of His children. Holy Spirit is Christ's presence in us. "Those who obey God's commandments remain in fellowship with him, and he with them. *And we know he lives in us because the Spirit he gave us lives in us*" (1 John 3:24 NLT, emphasis added). Here is what Paul says about the Holy Spirit in his letter to the Roman Christians: "The Spirit Himself bears witness with our spirit that we are children of God" (Romans 8:16 NKJV). If there is still any doubt in your mind as to the identity of the Holy Spirit, listen to the words of Jesus recorded in the Gospel of John. "However, when He, the Spirit of truth, has come, He will guide you into all truth; for He will not speak on His own authority, but whatever He hears He will speak; and He will tell you things to come" (John 16:13 NKJV). These three verses alone destroy the premise that the Holy Spirit is an it, a power, or an influence. He is the third person of the Trinity. God lives inside of us in the person of the Holy Spirit. Roll this thought around in your head for a moment. The same spirit who spoke all of creation into being breathed life into the first human, empowered men and women to do exploits, parted waters, opened blinded eyes, and raised the dead is the one who has taken up permanent residence in you. "The Spirit of God, who raised Jesus from the dead, lives in you. And just as God raised Christ Jesus from the dead, he will give life to your mortal bodies by this same Spirit living within you" (Romans 8:11 NLT).

The Father, the Word, and the Holy Spirit Are One

God came into the world in the person of the Holy Spirit to provide us with a constant source of courage and strength. The Holy Spirit is all-powerful (omnipotent), all-wise (omniscient), and everywhere present (omnipresent). There is only one God, eternally existing in three persons: Father, Son (Jesus Christ), and the Holy Spirit. The three persons of the Godhead are coequal and coeternal, one in essence, nature, power, action, and will (Genesis 1:26, Isaiah 9:6, Matthew 28:19–20, Luke 1:35, 1 John 2:20–23).

From internal evidence found in 1 John, it is safe to say this letter was addressed to a group of churches where *false prophets* had infiltrated with their denial of the incarnation of Jesus. Through his letter, John writes, "He who says." Someone in their fellowship was saying something. These false teachers were denying the Trinity. John exposed these feckless teachers to the truth of the Word of God. He nailed their coffins shut with these words: "For there are three that bear witness in heaven: *the Father, the Word*, and *the Holy Spirit*; and *these three are one*" (1 John 5:7 NKJV, emphasis added). Class is dismissed.

One of my favorite professors in seminary was Dr. Allen Henson. He taught systematic theology. The attrition rate in his classes was high, especially with first-semester students. He was very deep but fair. I left his class many times shaking my head and thinking, *What have I gotten myself into?* My GPA was going to tank. One day in class we were discussing the Trinity. We were all trying to adequately explain something that was inexplicable—the Holy Trinity. We were using illustrations like the egg. The egg is one but it consists of three parts: the shell, yoke, and white. Even though an egg has three parts, it is one.

Water was also used in an attempt to explain something that had no beginning—the Trinity. Water is a liquid, but it can be frozen to a solid. Water can also release steam when heat is applied. Water is one substance, but it can be expressed in three ways—liquid, solid, and steam. It never dawned on us that we were using something that had been created to explain the one who had created it, and we thought we were waxing eloquently. Dr. Henson was content with allowing us to make idiots out of ourselves. When the dialogue slowed, he said, "If you try to explain the Trinity, you will lose your mind. But if you deny it, you will lose your soul." I have never forgotten those wise words. At the end of the class, he gave us the best insight into the Holy Spirit that I'd ever heard before or since. I will share this insight with you in chapter 8.

Our Bodies Belong to God

It is impossible to own something that you did not create. Since you did not create your body, it does not belong to you. It belongs to your Creator. In his letter to the believers who lived in Corinth, Paul wrote these words, "All things are lawful for me, but all things are not helpful. All things are lawful for me, but I will not be brought under the power of any. Foods for the stomach and the stomach for foods, but God will destroy both it and them. Now *the body is not for sexual immorality but for the Lord*, and *the Lord for the body*. And God both raised up the Lord and will also raise us up by His power. Do you not know that *your bodies are members of Christ*? Shall I then take the members of Christ and make them members of a harlot? Certainly not! Or do you not know that he who is joined to a harlot is one body with her? For 'the two,' He says, 'shall become one flesh.' Flee sexual immorality. Every sin that a man does is outside the body, but he who commits sexual immorality sins against his own body. Or do you not know that *your body is the temple of the Holy Spirit who is in you*, whom you have from God and *you are not your own*" For you were bought with a price; therefore *glorify God in your body and in your spirit, which are God's*" (1 Corinthians 6:12–20 NKJV, emphasis added). God purchased you as His home when He paid for your life with His life.

The vast majority of humanity believes they can do whatever they like with their bodies. Their mantra is it's my body and I can do whatever I want with it. It was not, according to the Word of God. Your body is God's property. God breathed His spirit into you the moment you received Jesus Christ as your Lord and Savior; at that moment your body became a temple of God. Your body is His house. You're just the resident caretaker.

I find it fascinating that in the 1 Corinthians passage we just read, Paul compares the human body to the church; then later, he compares the church to the human body. The phrase "the body of Christ" is a common New Testament metaphor for the Church. Individually we are parts of the body; collectively we are one body. "The human body has many parts, but the many parts make up the whole body. So it is with the body of Christ. Yes, the body has many different parts, not just one part. All of you together are Christ's body, and each of you is a part of it" (1 Corinthians 12:12, 12:14, 12:27 NLT). The phrase "the body of Christ" is a reference to the church as a whole.

The apostle Paul penned these words to the Roman Christians, "Just as our bodies have many parts and each part has a special function, so it is with Christ's body. We are many parts of one body, and we all belong to each other" (Romans 12:4–5 NLT). "And He [Jesus] is the head of the body, the church, who is the beginning, the firstborn from the dead, that in all things He may have the preeminence" (Colossians 1:18 NKJV, emphasis added). Since we are His body, we don't have the freedom to do whatever we feel like doing. As an individual part of the body of Christ, we must be careful with what materials we use in building our lives on the foundation of Christ. Even though the body of Christ is made up of many members, we are in intimate union with the other parts of the body. What we do or don't do, not only affects us, it affects the entire body. "We are many parts of one body, and we all belong to each other" (Romans 12:5 NLT). The Church would be doing incredible exploits if it ever understood this truth about our new-creation identities: one body is made up of many parts.

God Is Still Breathing

The breath of God that hovered over a dark and formless world, the breath that spoke everything into existence, the breath that was breathed into the first human, the breath that was breathed upon the disciples, and the breath that was showered down in Acts 2 are the same breath that lives in us. He is our life (Colossians 3:4).

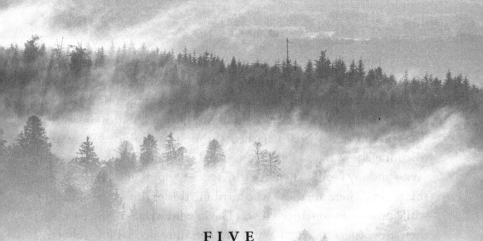

FIVE

Life and Death Are in Our Breaths

> The tongue can bring death or life; those who
> love to talk will reap the consequences.
> —PROVERBS 18:21 (NLT)

The power of words is unquestionable. Words are what brought all of creation into existence. In Genesis 1:11 (NKJV), God spoke and trees sprang up with life. In Mark 11:12–20 (NKJV), this same voice spoke and a fig tree withered and died. This proves how powerful spoken words can be. Words can give life or cause death. Can you imagine how many good things we may have killed in our own lives by the words we have spoken and are not even aware we have? If we really knew how creative words can be or how destructive words can be, I'm sure we would be more sensitive to what comes out of our mouths. We might breathe a little more cautiously if we knew that what we breathe out we will one day breathe in.

I read a very interesting article about self-talk recently. According to this short essay, the average person will talk to themselves at least 50,000 times a day! To be honest, the first thing I said to myself was "That can't be true." Surely no one has that much time to spend talking to themselves, especially if you have a habit of answering. Then Psalm 42:5 (NLT) flashed through my mind: "Why am I discouraged? Why is my heart so sad? I will praise Him again—my savior and my God!" There is a difference of opinion as to who wrote this psalm. There are those who attribute this psalm to the Korahites while others are convinced it was David who wrote it. Since I wasn't there to witness its writing and I'm certainly not a Bible scholar, I refuse to enter the fray over authorship. But there is one thing for certain, the individual who did write those words is definitely talking to themselves. "Even though I'm filled with discouragement and my soul is deeply sad, I choose to praise my savior and my God" (KniffKnotes). These words give credibility to the article I read on self-talk. We do talk to ourselves quite often. You are talking to yourself right now.

After meditating on the content of this article for a while, it began to dawn on me that before we make any decision, the first thing we do is engage ourselves in self-talk. "Do I turn on this street?" "What will I do if this doesn't turn out the way I'm hoping it will?" "What do I want to eat?" "How am I going to pay the repair bill on my vehicle?" "I wonder why my kids have not called?" "If that person says one more word, I'm going to"—you fill in the blank. Talking to ourselves 50,000 times a day may actually be a low number. It's unbelievable the amount of time we spend talking to ourselves. In one way I wish I had not read that article because now I find myself constantly monitoring the conversation that goes on between my ears. It is time-consuming and exhausting. If you think self-talk is not something relevant to you, start eavesdropping on the silent talk that is going on in your head—50,000 times a day.

After reading this article several times, I became a believer. We do spend a considerable amount of time in conversation with ourselves. What the writer of this article said next almost blew me out of my chair. Eighty percent of the time our self-talk is negative. If that is true and I have no reason to refute it, what we say to ourselves most often produces death. That is more earthshaking to me than talking to myself 50,000 times a day. That means that only 20 percent of the conversation we have with ourselves produces life. It stands to reason why the vast majority of humanity battles with anxiety, depression, loneliness, and a plethora of other negative emotions. We will eventually believe what we say—life or death.

This short essay I read ended with this statement: Ninety-five percent of our emotions are determined by the conversation we have within. It kind of sounds like the self-talk David was having with himself in Psalm 42 (NKJV), doesn't it? (I told you that I lean toward David's authorship of this psalm.) Since we are always engaging in self-talk, let's keep reminding ourselves that life and death are in our breaths.

The Importance of Breathing in Scripture

"How can a young person stay pure? By obeying your word. I have tried hard to find you—don't let me wander from your commands. *I have hidden your word in my heart,* that I might not sin against you" (Psalm 119:9–11 NLT, emphasis added). The truth of this verse is crystal clear to the honest reader. What we breathe in will determine how we live our daily lives. We are to hide the Word of God in our hearts, not in our heads. If God's Word is only in our heads, we have it, making it possible to be stolen. But when the Word of God is in our hearts, it has us, and it can never be poached.

Because we will breathe out whatever is in us, we should be cautious with what we breathe in. Remember the first scripture we started with? It was 2 Timothy 3:16 from The Passion Translation. This verse emphatically declares that God has transmitted His very substance, His essence, and His nature into the scriptures. This is what makes the written Word of God infallible. If we make it our priority to breathe in the Word of God when we exhale, we will be breathing out the very nature of God. The Word of God is truth therefore, our enemy who is a liar, has no weapon to defend himself against it. Paul calls the word the sword of the spirit (Ephesians 6:17 NKJV).

God's breath is the only thing that can impart life. "For the Spirit of God has made me, and *the breath of the Almighty gives me life*" (Job 33:4 NLT, emphasis added). "*In him* we live and move and exist" (Acts 17:28 NLT, emphasis added). The breath of God is His presence in us in the person of the Holy Spirit. Without God's breath in us, we have no lives.

We should be constantly breathing in the breath of God, so it will counteract all the negativity that unhealthy self-talk produces. Negative self-talk is the inner dialogue we have with ourselves that contradicts or limits our understanding of our newly created identities: who we are in Christ. Negative self-talk left unchecked can affect us in many damaging ways, ranging from minor feelings of inferiority to slavish depression. It can also sabotage our potential to be the more-than-conquerors Christ has made us to be (Romans 8:37 NKJV).

Enjoying the peace of God and the accompanying fruit of His peace does not come easily, nor is it obtained automatically. This is something that must be done on purpose. Paul addresses this very thing in his letter to the Philippians. "And now, dear brothers and sisters, one final thing. *Fix your thoughts* on what is true (God's Word), and honorable, and right, and pure, and lovely, and admirable. Think about things that are excellent and worthy of praise. *Keep putting into practice* all you learned and received from me—everything you heard from me and saw me doing. *Then the Peace of God will be with you*" (Philippians 4:8 NLT, emphasis added). We must become better stewards of the conversations we have within ourselves.

Seriously think about this. When we say things like "I am a loser," "I am no good," "I am pathetic," or "I am the lowest of lows," we are insinuating that God made a mistake when he created us. When God formed you in the secret place of your mother's womb, He created a masterpiece. God has never had to say oops when he created anything. Because God has never made a mistake, you are not His first. This is what negative self-talk really is. It is telling God that he fumbled the ball when he created us. This kind of negative talk is destructive, and it stymies our spiritual growth. The power of life and death being in our breaths cannot be exaggerated.

The Breath of God Will Stand Forever

When I became serious about my walk with Christ, I was blessed to be yoked up with a special mentor by the name of Lewis Bell. Lewis put his thumbprint on me in a special way. The first instruction he gave me was to internalize the Word of God in my deepest innermost being. That was the best instruction I have ever received. Every one of those scriptures that I hid in my heart is still as fresh today as they were then, and that was over fifty years ago. One of the scriptures I stowed away in my memory bank was one that described the written Word of God, "The grass withers, the flower fades, Because *the breath of the Lord* blows upon it. The grass withers, the flower fades, But *the word of God stands forever*" (Isaiah 40:7–8 NKJV, emphasis added). Pay attention to what Isaiah said about the Word of God. Everything will come to a screeching halt someday with the exception of the Word of God. It will continue forever. How is it possible for the Word of God to never end? The answer should be obvious by now. Since God is eternal (no beginning and no ending) and He has transmitted and breathed His very substance into the scriptures, His word must be eternal as well. Because God is holy and infallible, His word is holy and incapable of error as well. Every time we internalize a scripture, we are taking in more of God's breath. When we speak the Word of God, we are literally breathing the breath of God into our situations, including the face of our enemies. Internalizing God's Word is like stockpiling ammunition so we are adequately prepared for war. Lewis Bell knew this. He wanted me to be thoroughly equipped when I found myself engaged with the enemy who had no way of defending himself from God's breath—the sword of the spirit. What Lewis Bell imparted to me about the importance of storing up God's Word in my heart is what I try to impart to those young men I have the honor and privilege of mentoring.

The Breath of Death

The Word of God says that death is in the power of our breaths. The stakes are high. Death is present in our breaths. Our words can wreak destruction. This is why James gives us some godly counsel on being a good steward of what comes out of our mouths. "Understand this, my dear brothers and sisters: You must all be quick to listen, *slow to speak*, and slow to get angry" (James 1:19 NLT, emphasis added). It doesn't take a seminary graduate to understand what James is saying or means in this verse. We have two ears and one mouth, which means we are to do twice as much listening as speaking because our words usually lead to corresponding actions. "Watch your tongue and keep your mouth shut, and you will stay out of trouble" (Proverbs 21:23 NLT). I wonder what that means.

I'm sure that most of us in our growing up years heard this saying, "Sticks and stones may break my bones, but words will never hurt me" (Stephen Fry). Now that most of us have grown up, we know that is not true. Words can hurt. Words can break a person's spirit. A broken bone will heal in time, but oftentimes a person will carry their hurts and pains to the grave. Irreparable damage can be inflicted on a person's self-worth by negative words. Death and life are in our breaths.

There is another untruth that needs to be debunked. And it is this, there is no such thing as empty words. All words are filled with something. They are filled with life or they are filled with death. There are no amoral words. Every word that is released from our mouths is full of something. That something is our choice. The words we speak are loaded with life or they are impregnated with death.

My wife and I were engaged in a conversation about building people up with our words or tearing them down. Honestly I was tuning up my Sunday message by using her as a sounding board. I have never heard my wife say anything malicious or defamatory about anyone even those that I feel deserve it. Here's what she said, "I never want to say anything out of anger that I really don't mean. I can always say I'm sorry, but I can never take back those words." My wife, the theologian, sounds just like Jesus. "And I tell you this, you must give an account on judgment day for *every idle word* you speak" (Matthew 12:36 NLT). Words can cause festering wounds that never heal. If that does not slow our tongues down, I don't know what will.

The Breath of Life

Most young first-time parents wait with bated breath for their toddler to say their first word. They can get pretty giddy about it. It's not unusual for the mother and father to engage in light-hearted competition about which word their baby will say first. Will it be momma or dada? The winner will usually gloat and take a few victory laps. But I have witnessed relationships that became adversarial during this unique moment in time, for real. Just because we have grown older, it does not mean we have grown up: momma/dada.

The ability to speak is a gift from God. It is what separates us from all other animal forms. We are speaking spirits which makes us partakers of God's divine nature. "Then the Lord God formed man from the dust of the ground. *He breathed the breath of life into the man's nostrils*, and the man became a living person [a speaking spirit]" (Genesis 2:7 NLT, emphasis added). God breathed in so humanity could breathe out.

"A man has joy by the answer of his mouth. And *a word spoken in due season*, how good it is" (Proverbs 15:23 NKJV, emphasis added). Good timing is everything. This is what this verse in Proverbs is saying. A timely word spoken can build someone up; keep them from waving the white flag of surrender, throwing in the towel; or keep them from making foolish decisions. The creative power of the spoken word must never be underestimated. And we hold that power in our mouths. "*Winsome words* spoken at just the right time are as appealing as apples gilded in gold surrounded with silver" (Proverbs 25:11 TPT, emphasis added). When we share the written Word of God, we are in essence breathing out the breath of God, which has the ability to bring healing to an injured soul. "Nothing is more appealing than *speaking beautiful, love-giving words*. For they release sweetness to our souls and *inner healing to our spirits*" (Proverbs 16:24 TPT, emphasis added).

Speak Jesus

The scriptures emphatically declare that Jesus was the Word, and the Word was God. Then the Word became human, so we can say with certainty that Jesus is the very breath of God (John 1:1–2, 1:14 NLT). Let me state it the way I heard it in a theology class in seminary. This is the same class I mentioned in chapter 4. On this particular day, our class, filled with junior theologian wannabes, was making a flimsy attempt at defining the Trinity. Our professor gave us plenty of time to expose our lack of knowledge. When it was all said and done with help from Dr. Henson, here is what we left that class with as to who the Trinity is. Jesus is the human face of God-made flesh. The Holy Spirit is the breath (voice) of God expressed. That's not a bad definition when you are trying to explain the inexplicable. Every time the name Jesus leaves our lips, we breathe out the spirit of God that has the power to strengthen us in the middle of any circumstance no matter how difficult it may be. The name Jesus also has the power to transform our environments. Just say the name.

Here Be Lions, a collective group of Dustin Smith, Jesse Reeves, Charlene Prince, Raina Pratt, Kristen Dutton, and Abby Benton, teamed up to write the song "I Speak Jesus" in 2019. No one sings it better than Charity Gayle. It is one of those unique songs that can transform the way we look at life, as well as give us the strength and determination to subdue all the distractions that compete for our attention. I highly recommend that you listen to it if you haven't already. You might want to put it on loop play. To me, the following twenty-three words sum up the entire song.

Your name is power
Your name is healing
Your name is life
Break every stronghold
Shine through the shadows
Burn like a fire.

There is power in the name of Jesus. He is the Word and the Word was with God because He is God (John 1:1–5 NKJV). The universe was created with a word—speak Jesus. People were healed and demons were cast out with a word—speak Jesus. The dead were raised by a word—speak Jesus. Rulers and kingdoms have been taken down with a word—speak Jesus.

"Don't be selfish; don't try to impress others. Be humble, thinking of others as better than yourselves. Don't look out only for your own interests, but take an interest in others, too. *You must have the same attitude that Christ Jesus had. Though he was God*, he did not think of equality with God as something to cling to. Instead, *he appeared in human form*, he humbled himself in obedience to God and died a criminal's death on a cross" (Philippians 2:5–8 NLT, emphasis added). Speak Jesus.

The Choice of Life or Death

Speaking life or speaking death is a personal choice? If it is, then surely everyone will choose life, right? Wrong! You would think that would be an easy call, but the vast majority of humanity, past and present, have chosen death over life. It doesn't make any sense to a rational-thinking person that choosing death over life is the better option. If that happens to be your thoughts right now, let me ask you this question, what are you choosing? Life and death are in your breath.

Moses assembled the Israelites to review the terms of the covenant God had made with them. In this covenant review, Moses reminds the Israelites what God told them about life and death. It's in the power of the tongue. The tongue can speak life, or it can speak death. It is absolutely staggering how much power is in our mouths. If we really knew, we would guard with great care what we say. "Today *I have given you the choice between life and death*, between blessings and curses. Now I call on heaven and earth to witness the choice you make. *Oh, that you would choose life*, so that you and your descendants might live" (Deuteronomy 30:19 NLT, emphasis added). Just in case you are vacillating between what choice to make, I highly suggest you choose life. I'm just saying.

Have you ever had someone's acid tongue burn you? Has your acid tongue ever burned anyone? Have kind words ever refreshed your soul? Have you ever refreshed someone's soul with your kind words? I would bet that every honest person would have to fess up to having done both. In the Book of Wisdom, we find these words: "*When you speak healing words*, you offer others fruit from the tree of life. But *unhealthy, negative words do nothing but crush their hopes*" (Proverbs 15:4 TPT, emphasis added).

I am convinced that a person who has a hard time controlling one's tongue has an integrity issue. You can rest assured that if an individual cannot control their mouths, they will have other uncontrolled issues as well. Maybe that's why the Word of God tells us to be quick to hear but slow to speak (James 1:19 NLT). A spiritually mature person is one who has learned to control the breath they choose to breathe out because they know they carry the power of life and death in their words.

I do realize there are occasions when we slip on our own tongues and say things we wish we had not said. When that happens, we oftentimes say that we had a Freudian slip. That usually gets us off the hook. Most of the time. In fifty years of preaching and ministering the word, I have had my share of red-faced moments that I created by misspeaking. I am sure there are probably more of those uncomfortable occasions waiting to ambush me in the future.

When the Cross Breathed

Hanging on the cross with both arms outstretched and hands nailed to a wooden beam, Jesus cried, "It is finished" (John 19:30 NKJV). Then He bowed His head and released His spirit. Jesus breathed out His life so we would have the opportunity to breathe in His life. This moment in time says it all.

God demonstrated His love for us by sending His Son Jesus Christ to die in our place on an old rugged cross while we were still in our sinning states. God loved us when we did not want anything to do with Him (Romans 5:8 NKJV). In essence, Jesus's dying on the cross was the ultimate expression of the Father's love for us. You, my beloved, are of inestimable value to our heavenly Father. The next time you find yourself battling unworthiness, self-condemnation, depression, or hopelessness, remember Jesus chose to die rather than live without you. Since Jesus died so we can live, let's live for Him.

SIX

Refreshed by God's Breath

The Lord grant mercy to the household of Onesiphorus, for
he often refreshed me, and was not ashamed of my chain.
—2 TIMOTHY 1:16 (NKJV)

There is not a person alive who at some point in time does not need to be refreshed by a timely word of encouragement. The world is relentless with its demands for our time and attention. Our emotional energy and spiritual vitality can be drained out slowly oftentimes before we are even aware that we are losing momentum. The enemy's constant bombardments with distractions and false priorities can cause us to hoist the white flag of surrender. The devil and the kingdom of darkness are committed to wearing out the children of God (Daniel 7:25 NKJV). As long as we are in our dirt suits (physical bodies), we will get physically exhausted and emotionally tired. If we never have a time of refreshing, we may throw in the towel. A lot of incredible people filled with giftings and potential have given up because they grew weary and fatigued, especially if they have been engaged in spiritual warfare for an extended period of time. How many people do you know who were once on fire for God, but now you can't find them even with the help of the FBI or the CIA? Maybe that person is you. No one is exempt from burnout no matter how tough they may appear to be.

There is a direct correlation between the body and the soul. If one gets off-kilter, it can affect the other. Physical stress can steal our emotional strength, and emotional weariness can lead to physical complications. Paul wrote these words to Gaius, a faithful member of the community of faith who had a heart for hospitality. He always had the welcome mat out for any weary traveling servant of the Lord. They always had a place at his table. "Beloved, I pray that you may prosper in all things and *be in health, just as your soul prospers*" (3 John 1:2 NKJV, emphasis added). Pay close attention to the connection John makes between the body and soul. If one is unhealthy, there is the potential for it to cause the other part to be infirm. Physical struggles can affect our minds, emotions, and wills. Negative thoughts and feelings can eventually take their toll on our bodies.

There Are No Exemptions

This may be hard to believe, but there were seasons in the apostle Paul's life when he needed to be refreshed. There is no doubt that Paul was a spiritual giant. That incredible man of God wrote over half of the New Testament. Paul was not afraid to get in the face of someone who was not living up to their calling in Christ. He was not hesitant to confront Peter when he was compromising the truth of the Gospel message (Galatians 2:11–21 NLT). Paul faced down rulers and exposed the synagogue hierarchy for their hypocrisy. Paul was unafraid. You would think someone with this much spunk and vinegar would never need someone to lift their spirits. But he did. His friend Onesiphorus was given that assignment. His name says it all. It means benefit-bringing, or profit-bearing. He certainly lived up to his name. That is exactly what he was to Paul. He was useful and profitable. God used Onesiphorus to keep Paul on his feet, to put a fresh wind in his emotional sails. In keeping with the theme of this book, let me state it this way: God breathed through Onesiphorus the strength Paul needed to keep going when exhaustion was taking its toll. Never ever underestimate the power that your timely word has on someone who desperately needs to hear it. God wants to breathe through you a word in season that will keep someone from throwing up their hands and surrendering. We will never know on this side of eternity how many people were able to finish their race simply because God used us to give them a timely word. A timely word is just that—it's timely. "Everyone enjoys a fitting reply; it is wonderful to say the right thing at the right time!" (Proverbs 15:23 NLT).

A Timely, In-Season Word

Is there a difference between a timely word and a word spoken in season? That is a legitimate question that begs to be answered. I would say that these words are probably kissing cousins, but I also think there may be a subtle difference between the two that is worth pointing out. This may be splitting hairs, but this is how I see the distinction between *a timely word* and *a word in season*.

A *timely word* is just that, it is timely. A life-imparting word spoken at just the right moment has the power to change everything. It strengthens feeble knees; it gives hope to the hopeless, joy to the saddened, and life to the lifeless. A timely word can keep a person going when everything inside of them is squalling for them to quit. Never ever underestimate the value of a word spoken at just the right moment.

A *word in season* comes when we find ourselves in the middle of an episode in our lives that is slowly draining our physical and spiritual energy. We are not going under yet, but we are getting tired from treading water. A word given to us in this season renews our strength and keeps us afloat. A word in due season is a life jacket that keeps us from drowning. It corresponds with the season we are going through.

We all need an Onesiphorus in our lives. If we don't have one, we can be one. Intentionally be the kind of person who puts fresh wind in the sail of someone who has drifted off course because words of death and negativity have been spoken about them, or over them. The power of life and death are in the words we speak (Proverbs 18:21 NKJV).

We were not created to do life alone. This is why the Word of God says that collectively we are the body of Christ (1 Corinthians 12:12–14 NKJV). There is only one body, but the body has many members. Every member does what it is designed for to make sure the body is healthy and functioning properly. God gave me what you need to make that happen, and He gave you what I need. Alone, we become the enemy's chattel. There are a lot of people who are tittering on the precipice of surrender. To keep them from giving up, turning loose, and letting go, let's choose to be an Onesiphorus. Let the Lord breathe His breath through you on those who have lost hope. One timely word, one word in due season, can reinvigorate a person who has lost all hope of accomplishing their divine assignment in life. The bar ditch in life is littered with individuals who have lost their spiritual wind.

The Breath of God May Come in a Still Small Voice

Sometimes our greatest need is to have some cave time alone—a time to rest, a time to heal, a time to gather our scattered thoughts, and a time for personal reflection just like Elijah had (1 Kings 19:9 NKJV). There is not a person alive who does not need a quiet season so they can hear God's voice (Psalm 46:10 NKJV). God can use these cave-time moments to breathe fresh hope into us. This renewed strength will usually come in a still small voice. We must be vigilant, because if we allow ourselves to be distracted, we may miss the very thing our soul is crying out for.

One of the greatest prophets who has ever lived received new strength while he was hunkered down in the confines of a cave. With no TV, radio, iPad, cell phone, or anything else that would distract him, Elijah was able to hear the voice of God in a fresh new way. This was on the heels of doing great exploits for God. He now finds himself on the run. Jezebel sent word to Elijah that within twenty-four hours his fate would be the same as were the eight hundred fifty prophets of Baal. Every one of them had been executed at the Brook of Kishon (1 Kings 18:40 NKJV). Jezebel had wanted posters for Elijah's death distributed all over the region. This prophet of God was a dead man.

"And when he (Elijah) *saw that*, he arose and *ran for his life*, and went to Beersheba, which belongs to Judah, and left his servant there (1 Kings 19:3 NKJV, emphasis added). What jumps out of this verse screaming for attention is Elijah had a visual of what Jezebel had said. This validates the truth that words can and do paint pictures. The message that was sent to Elijah was verbal, but he saw what had been said. He was so distraught that he asked God to kill him. "But he himself went a day's journey into the wilderness, and came and sat down under a broom tree. And *he prayed that he might die*, and said, 'It is enough! Now, Lord, *take my life*, for I am no better than my fathers'" (1 Kings 19:4 NKJV, emphasis added).

When a person gets mentally exhausted, they are apt to say things they really do not mean. If Elijah had really wanted to die, he would not have run away so fast. Jezebel would have gladly obliged him. Mental exhaustion can lead to physical collapse and spiritual burnout. But burnout is only permanent if you allow it to be. All it takes to quench the fire that is trying to consume us is for God to breathe fresh life into us. And most of the time our refreshing moments will come when God speaks to us in a still small voice (1 Kings 19:12 NKJV). This is why it is imperative for us to be still during hectic times. Quiet waiting enables us to hear and smell the breath of God. Instead of running from God, we need to be sitting at His feet. It was God's breath that put Elijah back on His feet. Psalm 46:10 is true today as it was when it was penned: "Be still and know that I am God" (Psalm 46:10 NKJV). The word *still* in

Hebrew means *to relax*. It carries the idea of something falling off when we obey this command. That's right, being still is a command from God, not a suggestion. In relaxing moments with Him, our anxiety, striving, stress, preoccupation, and the cares of this life drop off. What had been weighing us down is lifted when we obey this command.

God will not compete with all the distractions swirling around us. This is why it is so easy for us not to hear Him when He speaks. He will not try to outshout all the other voices that are screaming for our attention. The loudest voice we hear may not be the voice we need to be listening to during our moments of physical, emotional, and spiritual exhaustion. It is wise to keep our mouths shut and both ears open.

Let's take a closer look at what happened when Elijah was placed in time-out. Fear had squeezed the life out of this prophet of God. The scriptures do not say that we should not feel fear. They say we are not to be afraid. The difference between feeling fear and being afraid is control. When we feel fear, we are still in control. When we are afraid, fear is controlling us. Elijah had gone from feeling fear to being afraid. Fear is now calling the shots in what choices he made. This is why he chose to run and not fight. This is so out of character for Elijah. He was a seasoned combatant. What happened? When we are in the throes of fear, we may find ourselves doing what we said we would never do and saying things we never dreamed we would say. Don't ever underestimate the power fear can have over your life. This mighty prophet of God had surrendered to *a spirit* of fear (2 Timothy 1:7 NLT). Fear will take the fight out of you.

God's Gentile Whisper

No matter how far fear may have knocked you down, all it takes is a little puff of God's breath to put you back on your feet. The breath of God is life. He spoke to Elijah in a still small voice, a gentle whisper, and Elijah heard it. Our heavenly Father is still speaking to His children in a soft gentle voice. If we are not careful all of the distractions swirling around will drum out our ability to hear what we so desperately need, and that is the sound of God's voice. He is the only one who has the power to resuscitate us when we feel like death has won. He is also the only one who can strengthen our feeble knees. Never underestimate the power that is in the gentile whisper of God's breath.

> "Go out and stand before me on the mountain, the Lord told him [Elijah]. And as Elijah stood there, the Lord passed by, and a mighty windstorm hit the mountain. It was such a terrible blast that the rocks were torn loose, but the Lord was not in the wind. After the wind there was an earthquake, but the Lord was not in the earthquake. And after the earthquake there was a fire, but the Lord was not in the fire. And after the fire there was *the sound of a gentle whisper. When Elijah heard it,* he wrapped his face in his cloak and went out and stood at the entrance of the cave." (1 Kings 19:11–13 NLT, emphasis added)

Elijah saw the wind, but he did not hear the voice of God. He also saw and felt the earthquake, but he did not hear the voice of God. This mighty prophet saw the fire, but he did not hear the voice of God. He heard God speak when he was still and quiet.

I guess it would be safe to say that God will not speak to us in the wind. I think Jonah would beg to differ with us about that (Jonah 1:4 NKJV). Will God speak to us in the midst of an earthquake? Elijah did not hear His voice when the earth shook under his feet. But don't try to convince Paul and Silas that God can't be heard in the middle of an earthquake (Acts 16: 25–26 NKJV). If God's voice cannot be heard in the wind and the earthquake, then it stands to reason His voice cannot be heard in the fire either. Well, Moses, Shadrach, Meshach, and Abednego may have something to say about that (Exodus 3:1–5, Daniel 3:19–27 NKJV).

God can speak to us in any way He chooses. It may take a storm for Him to get our undivided attention. He certainly got Jonah's attention. At other times, it may take an earthquake to shake us loose from the things we are clinging to for security. There are times when we may need a control burn. The peace we have is knowing that God does not send a fire to destroy us. It is for the purpose of purifying and burning away the clutter we have become attached to so we can hear His voice.

Elijah was physically, emotionally, and spiritually spent. What he needed more than anything else was a time of refreshing. He desperately needed some fresh wind put back into his spiritual sails. This is what happens when we obey God's command, "*Be still*, and know that I am God" (Psalm 46:10 NKJV, emphasis added).

Relaxing at the Feet of Jesus

If there is any one word that adequately describes our lives today, it is the word busy. We are busy people. We have become very efficient in how to be really busy when we're busy. Our day usually starts early, and we plopped into bed late at night tired and exhausted. After a short night's sleep, we repeat the previous day. Is there any wonder we suffer from burnout? I call this the Martha syndrome. I will explain why in just a moment.

There is nothing wrong with having a schedule full of activities. We just need to make sure we are in control of our busy schedules. If our schedules start taking control of our lives, we will gradually lose our momentum. Burnout is real. If we push hard enough for long enough, it will not take long before we become physically frazzled, emotionally drained, and spiritually exhausted. This is why it is imperative for us to take the time to spend time at the Lord's feet. We need to purposely seek out some cave time for ourselves, so we can smell the breath of our heavenly Father and have Him breathe on us.

One of the best stories to illustrate what relaxing at the feet of Jesus looks like is the one about two sisters named Mary and Martha. "As Jesus and his disciples continued on their way to Jerusalem, they came to a certain village where a woman named Martha welcomed him into her home. Her sister, *Mary, sat at the Lord's feet, listening to what he taught.* But *Martha was distracted* by the big dinner she was preparing. She came to Jesus and said, 'Lord, doesn't it seem unfair to you that my sister sits here while I do all the work? Tell her to come and help me.' But the Lord said to her, 'My dear Martha, you are worried and upset over all these details! *There is only one thing worth being concerned about. Mary has discovered it*, and it will not be taken away from her'" (Luke 10:38–42 NLT, emphasis added). Martha was busy in the kitchen preparing a meal. That was a good thing. Mary was relaxing at the feet of Jesus. That was the best thing. What Jesus said about Mary grabs my attention. She had discovered the most important thing, and that was being still in the presence of the Lord. This brings Psalm 46:10 back in focus, "Be still, and know that I am God" (NKJV). Martha was working. Mary was worshipping. We will work better when we worship first.

I certainly do not want to disparage those who are hard workers. The community of faith does not have enough of these incredible people who are willing to roll up their sleeves and go to work. We certainly need more Martha's. We find three types of people in the church today: "Those who make things happen, those who watch things happen, and those who wonder what happened" (Nicholas Murray Butler). Martha was one of those who made it happen.

But somehow we have lost our way when it comes to work and worship. Worship must always precede work. Why is that? When we spend time at the feet of Jesus, basking in His presence, we regain our spiritual energy and strength. We get recharged. The breath of God refreshes us. A refreshed and recharged child of God becomes a very dependable worker.

Last Day Refreshing

Being a minister of the Gospel of Christ can be the most euphoric experience ever, or it can be the biggest nightmare of one's life. There is so much misconception about the life of someone who is in full-time ministry or a sold-out believer. The constant demand to do things bigger and better can take a good-meaning person to an early grave. What is found in the pulpit can also be found in the pews: burned out, tired, discouraged, and depressed children of God. We have worked hard, but we have not spent enough time like Mary, sitting at the feet of Jesus quietly and listening.

One of my biggest ministries at this juncture in life is refreshing pastors, men, and women of God who have become disillusioned with ministry and flamed out. They can't see the possibility of ever recovering. Those who once flexed their strengths and fought the good fight of faith have waved the white flag of surrender. In every case, without exception, work over worship has been the culprit. Worshipping God is how we get the strength to do the work of God. If this order is ever reversed, it's not a matter of if we quit, it's when.

Ever since God breathed out in Genesis 1 and man breathed in in Genesis 2, there has never been a time when humankind has not needed to be refreshed by God's breath. But even more so in this last season. The battle to gain control over our lives has intensified. The conflict we find ourselves in for spiritual survival is no longer a skirmish. It is now a full-blown battle. Our need to be refreshed by the breath of God cannot be overstated in this last-day season.

"You will keep him in perfect peace, whose mind is stayed on You, because he trusts in You" (Isaiah 26:3 NKJV). Worship is how we keep our minds focused on the main thing. The fruit will be perfect peace. Maybe a little more personal cave time would be a tremendous help. Elijah sure benefitted from his personal time out with God.

"For in him we live and move and exist" (Acts 17:28 NLT). I'm certainly not a biblical scholar by any stretch of the imagination, but this verse sounds to me like we cannot do anything without God. Since this is true, why wouldn't we want to spend more time relaxing in His presence? These special moments provide opportunities for us to hear, feel, and smell the breath of our Creator. When God breathes out, we breathe in. If God ever stopped breathing, everything would come to a screeching halt. "He existed before anything else, and he holds all creation together" (Colossians 1:17 NLT). How does God hold all things together? The answer is simple, by His breath.

"By faith we understand that the entire universe was formed at God's command [breath], that what we now see did not come from anything that can be seen" (Hebrews 11:3 NLT). The breath of God spoke all of creation into order, and it remains in order because He is still breathing.

SEVEN

It Is Time to Breathe in Some Fresh Air

Every part of Scripture, is God-breathed and useful one way or another—showing us truth, exposing our rebellion, correcting our mistakes, training us to live God's way. Through the Word we are put together and shaped up for the tasks God has for us.
—2 TIMOTHY 3:16–17 (TPT)

The time came when my wife and I purchased a building in our small town so she would have a permanent place for her lady's boutique. We had been renting a space for about twelve years when we felt it was time for us to step out and see our dreams fulfilled. I have always had an itch to take an old building and renovate it. I was about to get the opportunity to scratch that itch.

The building we bought was built in 1917. My goal was to make it look as much like it did when it was built as I possibly could. When I removed the dropped ceiling tile, I found a treasure. The original building had a twenty-foot stamped tin ceiling that was in mint condition. The place really began to pop once I removed the old plaster that had been smeared over the beautiful antique bricks. Exposing those gorgeous interior brick walls may have been one of the better decisions I made in the entire renovation project. Like the beautiful ceilings, they were in pristine condition. The possibilities to make this building really special were endless.

It took a lot of patience and sweat equity to make this happen. When it came time to prepare the concrete for installing wood flooring, I rented a commercial buffer that had a diamond head attachment. This was the most effective way to remove the one-hundred-year-old stains and glue from years past. This buffer was a beast. But there was one thing I overlooked. I did not take into consideration the dust that would be created when the buffing began. Can you say dust?

Even though I wore eye protection and a respirator, it could not protect me from the amount of dust being generated by the buffer. I had several people tell me that they came by to see how things were going, but when they opened the door, they could hear the buffer but could not see me. There were moments when I was forced to take a break. The dust would become overpowering. My lungs would be screaming for fresh air. There were times when I actually went into panic mode. I would shut the buffer off and run out the back door of the building as fast as I could. Once outside, I would rip off my safety glass and respirator so I could breathe in some fresh air. The outside air was refreshing and invigorating. It felt so good to be able to breathe without coughing. Being able to take in oxygen took away the panic that had taken control of my breathing, forcing me to quit. Once refreshed, I returned to buffing the concrete floors; only to repeat my escape routine time and time again. I am glad to report that I did finish buffing the concrete and installing the wooden floors. What kept me going were the moments when I made the decision to breathe fresh air into my lungs. One big gulp of air did not take away my need for more oxygen. To be able to breathe so I could finish my task at hand required that I stop what I was doing and purposefully breathe in fresh air. Without the ability to breathe, I was toast.

At times life can be like a buffer with a diamond head attachment. It grinds really well, but it can also create an atmosphere that will challenge our survival. This is why we will always need quiet time to breathe in some fresh air.

Jesus Breathed out so We Could Breathe In

The reason most believers fly high one day and bottom out the next is that they do not spend enough alone time in the Word of God. The word was given to be our daily bread, not just for special occasions like Easter and Christmas. Is there any wonder why the community of faith is so malnourished? Only the scriptures have the nourishment we need to be spiritually healthy. This is why Jesus told us to make our home in the Word (John 8:31–32 NKJV). For in it, we will know the truth, and the truth we know will not only set us free, but it will keep us free.

During Jesus's wilderness temptation, the devil tried to get Him to focus on physical bread in order to get His needs met. Jesus said, "It is written, Man shall not live by bread alone, but by every word that proceeds from the mouth of God" (Matthew 4:4 NKJV). Jesus did not deny our need for physical bread. Food is necessary for our survival. He was putting things in the right perspective. Physical needs are real, but they must never become a substitute for what we really need. And that is to have the spiritual hunger of our souls satisfied. Jesus is the only one who can meet that need.

Humanity can only survive and thrive by what comes out of the mouth of God—His breath. This is why John recorded Jesus's words in his Gospel, "*I am the living bread* which came down from heaven. If anyone eats of this bread, *he will live forever*; and the bread that I shall give is My flesh, which I shall give for the life of the world" (John 6:51 NKJV, emphasis added). The Word became flesh and lived among humankind. Jesus is the only bread that has the power to give everlasting life. The German philosopher Ludwig Feuerbach was spot on when he said, "We are what we eat." If that is true (and it is), then living our spiritual lives undernourished is a choice we make.

Jeremiah, the Old Testament weeping prophet, also stressed our need for ingesting the Word of God. Pay close attention to what Jeremiah said he had eaten and what it produced in his life. *"Your words were found, and I ate them, and Your word was to me the joy and rejoicing of my heart*; For I am called by Your name, O Lord God of hosts" (Jeremiah 15:16 NKJV, emphasis added). Jeremiah consumed the words of God, and they became the source of pleasure and happiness in his life. The word (breath) of God gives us what our hearts long for, happiness and contentment. Now we know why Jesus said what he said to the crowd who had been blessed with an all-you-can-eat fish and chip meal: "Most assuredly, I say to you, he who believes in Me has everlasting life. Your fathers ate the manna [bread] in the wilderness, and are dead. This is the bread which comes down from heaven, that one may eat of it and not die. *I am the living bread* which came down from heaven. If anyone eats of this bread, he will live forever; and the bread that I shall give is My flesh, which I shall give for the life of the world" (John 6:47–51 NKJV, emphasis added). You are what you eat. Need I say anymore?

Jesus breathed His last breath on an old bloody cross, so we would have the opportunity to breathe our first breath as new creation beings. "After this, knowing that all things were now accomplished, that the Scripture might be fulfilled, said, 'I thirst!' Now a vessel full of sour wine was sitting there; and they filled a sponge with sour wine, put it on hyssop, and put it to His mouth. So when Jesus had received the sour wine, He said, *'It is finished!'* And bowing His head, *He gave up His spirit*" (John 19:28–30 NKJV, emphasis added). Jesus did not say that He was finished when He breathed His last breath. He was declaring that everything He came to earth to do for humanity had been accomplished. Everything that fallen humanity needed to have the opportunity to be in the right standing with God had been completed. The Living Word, the Living Bread from heaven, paid the price for the only meal that can provide what every human soul cries out for—grace and truth (John 1:14 NKJV).

Our newly created lives are powered by the breath of God. Let me say something that I have already said a couple of times. Jesus breathed out so we could breathe in. "And Jesus cried out with a loud voice, and *breathed His last*." "So when the centurion, who stood opposite Him, saw that He cried out like this and *breathed His last*, he said, 'Truly this Man was the Son of God'" (Mark 15:37–39 NKJV, emphasis added). "And when Jesus had cried out with a loud voice, He said, 'Father, into Your hands I commit my spirit.' Having said this, *He breathed His last*" (Luke 23:46 NKJV, emphasis added). This is God demonstrating how much He loves humanity. "But God demonstrated His own love toward us, in that while we were still sinners, Christ died for us" (Romans 5:8 NKJV). Never, never, never question God's love for you.

God designed our physical bodies with the ability to inhale oxygen and exhale carbon dioxide. This helps to keep us healthy and alive. What is true in our physical lives is even more true when it comes to our spiritual lives. As new creations, we have the ability to breathe out our worries so we can breathe in His peace. We can breathe out fear so we can breathe in His faith. We can breathe out anxiety so we can breathe in His trust. You can write your own breathe-out-breathe-in sentences. As a matter of fact, why don't you do that right now? Ready? Breathe out _____ so we can breathe in His _____ .

Jesus and the Holy Spirit: Going and Coming

The Holy Spirit could not come until Jesus ascended back to heaven. Jesus had to go before the Holy Spirit could come. The following are the words Jesus spoke to His disciples, "But now *I go away* to Him who sent Me, and none of you asks Me, 'Where are You going?' But because I have said these things to you, sorrow has filled your heart. Nevertheless, I tell you the truth. *It is to your advantage that I go away*; for if I do not go away, *the Helper* [Holy Spirit] *will not come to you*; but *if I depart*, I will send *Him* to you" (John 16:5–7 NKJV, emphasis added). This conversation between Jesus and His disciples took place before He was crucified on the cross. His death and resurrection had not taken place yet. Jesus made it very clear that for the Holy Spirit to come into the earthly realm, He had to depart and return to the heavenly realm back to His Father. Let me point out one thing before we move on. Jesus told His disciples that once He departed, He would send the helper whom He referred to as Him. I've said this already, but it needs to be said again. Every child of God needs to understand that the Holy Spirit is not an it, a power, or an influence. The Holy Spirit is a person. He is God's present to us and God's presence in us.

After Jesus was crucified on the cross, after He breathed His last breath, and after He conquered death and left the grave, He appeared to His disciples who were huddled behind locked doors trembling in fear. They were about to learn that no shut door could keep out the presence of Christ. This unexpected encounter with the resurrected Christ caught everyone off guard even though they had been told by eyewitnesses that He was alive. They thought everything was over. All of their hopes and dreams had been buried with Jesus. Then all of a sudden, He was in the same room with them. No wonder Jesus said, "Peace be with you" (John 20:19 NKJV). I'm sure they were pretty rattled by His sudden appearance. Here is an interesting sidenote that I think is very important. This event took place during the evening hours, and it was a private meeting between Jesus and His disciples. I am convinced that this is the connecting link between John 20:22 and Acts 2 that helps us understand what Jesus said to His disciples. "The Spirit of truth, whom the world cannot receive, because it neither sees Him nor knows Him; but you know Him, for He *dwells with you* and *will be in you*" (John 16:17

NKJV, emphasis added). In all the years that I have read this verse, I have not slowed down enough to pay attention to what Jesus actually said. He told the disciples that the Holy Spirit was *with them,* but the time was coming when the Holy Spirit would be *in them.* I bet some readers are beginning to connect the dots. Once again Jesus refers to the Holy Spirit as Him.

The Two Encounters

What took place behind closed doors happened at night. What took place in Acts 2 happened during the day. One meeting was private, and one was public. Both events were focused on the imparting of the spirit of God. Since the nighttime encounter the disciples had with Jesus happened before Pentecost, we will begin there.

"*Then he* [Jesus] *breathed on them* and said, 'Receive the Holy Spirit'" (John 20:22 NLT, emphasis added). This verse is screaming for attention. Has Jesus forgotten what He told His disciples earlier? He had not ascended yet, and He said the Holy Spirit could not come until He left. What Jesus said and what He did appears to be in contradiction with what actually happened. He said He had to leave before the Holy Spirit could come. I tell people all of the time that when there appears to be a contradiction in the scriptures, that is exactly what you have—an appearance.

In my fifty years in ministry, I have heard some persuasive apologetics given by brilliant men over these two spirit impartations. In no way would I ever claim to be in the same league with these biblical scholars or even close. I'm just a simple country boy trying to figure things out. The more I learn, the little I see that I know. In spite of that, I will share with you what my understanding is of these two events.

I hang my hat on the linchpin of the night and day distinction between the two events. To me it really does not matter if someone sees the John 20 account as a partial enduement of power in the prelude to the outpouring of the Holy Spirit in Acts 2. Many theologians do. At the same time, there are just as many who contend that what Jesus did with His disciples was a prophetic parable pointing toward Pentecost. This too has some credibility. I will give everyone the freedom to come to their own conclusion concerning these two events. Knowing the difference does not make you more of a child of God, and not knowing does not make you less than a child of God.

Private Meeting

Let's take a closer look at the private meeting Jesus had with His disciples when He breathed on them and told them to receive the Holy Spirit. After we look at this private moment between the disciples and Jesus, we will take a gander at that incredible daytime moment when God breathed out His Spirit on the masses, and they were filled with His eternal presence. Once again, one event was private and took place at night. The other one was public and took place during the day.

There are a lot of things we do not know, but there is one thing for certain: the mission that Jesus came to inaugurate was intended to be perpetual. He was sent to impact humanity with the love of God and to give all of humankind the opportunity to be restored from where they fell in Genesis 3. For this to happen, it would require the empowerment of the Holy Spirit. Jesus was able to accomplish His earthly assignment by the power and anointing of the Holy Spirit that resided inside of Him, and that was the only way the church would continue this divine assignment that we were commissioned to carry out.

We need to slowly walk our way through this proposition, and to do that, we need to lay some groundwork that will help guide us to the answers we are pursuing. Let me propose the first question that we need to answer. How many Gods are there? I use the capital

G to give this question more punch. Most Christians do not hesitate with their answer: There is only one God. This is the correct answer too because we have scripture to support that claim. "To you it was shown, that you might know that *the Lord Himself is God; there is none other besides Him*" (Deuteronomy 4:35 NKJV, emphasis added). "Therefore know this day, and consider it in your heart, that *the Lord Himself is God in heaven above and on the earth beneath; there is no other*" (Deuteronomy 4:39 NKJV, emphasis added). "Hear, O Israel: The Lord our God, *the Lord is one!*" (Deuteronomy 6:4 NKJV, emphasis added). I think the Word of God establishes the fact that there is only one God, and He has no competition or challengers.

This brings me to the second question that needs to be addressed. Who was God talking to when he was creating humanity? "Then God said 'Let *Us* make man in *Our image*, according to *Our likeness*; let them have dominion over the fish of the sea, over the birds of the air, and over the cattle, over all the earth and over every creeping thing that creeps on the earth'" (Genesis 1:26 NKJV, emphasis added). The answer to this question does not come as fast as the answer to the first question we posed. The pause in answering is not because we do not believe there is one God. It's because we have not given much time (if any) to think our way through this second question. Could it be that God was talking to Himself? I personally think He was. If you think talking to one's self is kind of weird, then I suggest you eavesdrop on the next conversation you have with yourself. We all do.

Since the Bible unequivocally confirms the fact that there is only one God, then how do we explain God the Father, God the Son, and God the Holy Spirit? To many people, it may seem like there are three Gods, not one. In no way am I going to try to explain the Holy Trinity, but I will take you back to Dr. Henson's systematic theology class that I mentioned in chapter 4. Even though it has been many, many years since my seminary days, I still remember what he said to us students one day as we were discussing the Trinity, "If you try to explain the Holy Trinity, you will lose your mind. If you deny the Holy Trinity, you will lose your soul." I would lay odds that what my professor said to us young preacher boys in his class that day will never escape your memory either. Lose your mind, or lose your soul. The choice is yours.

What you are about to read is what Dr. Henson shared with us students years ago about the Holy Trinity written in my words from the notes I took in his class. Take your time. Read slowly, prayerfully, and meditatively.

God has chosen to reveal Himself through three distinct personalities. He is God the Father, He is God the Son, and He is God the Holy Spirit. In all three expressions of His divine being, He never ceases to be God.

This raises a third question that begs to be answered. Who is Jesus? Is He God or the Son of God? Let's get our answer from the Holy Scriptures. After all, God's Word is His breath, and since He never changes, His Word will never change either.

Let's begin our pursuit to find the answer in the Gospel of John. "In the beginning was the Word, and *the Word was with God*, and *the Word was God*. He [Word] was in the beginning with God. All things were made through Him, and without Him nothing was made that was made" (John 1:1–3 NKJV, emphasis added). In this passage of scripture, Jesus is presented as the Word. The Word (Jesus) was in the beginning with God. The Word was God, and everything was made through Him. Maybe this is who God was talking to when He said, "[Then God said], 'Let US make man in Our image, according to Our likeness'" (Genesis 1:26 NKJV). Logical inductive reasoning affirms that the Word in John 1:14 is Jesus. This theological position is easily defended, and I am convinced it cannot be disproven. "God was in Christ (incarnation) reconciling the world to Himself, not imputing their trespasses to them, and has given us the word of reconciliation" (2 Corinthians 5:19 NKJV, emphasis added).

John is not through with His introduction of the Word. "And the Word became flesh and dwelt among us, and we beheld His glory, the glory as of the only begotten of the Father, full of grace and truth" (John 1:14 NKJV). In our Christian faith, this is called the incarnation: God wrapped himself up in human form in the body of Jesus—who is the Word. This is the union of divinity with humanity. The Word became flesh and dwelt among us.

There is a fourth question that should be obvious now. Who is the Holy Spirit? In no way am I making the claim that I have insight into the Trinity that no one else has. The Trinity is beyond logic. What you are about to read requires an open mind and a teachable spirit. It has the potential to make you feel uncomfortable at first, but keep reading. My prayer is that this will give you some insight into how one God can manifest himself through three distinct personalities. I would encourage you to read it several times slowly, prayerfully, and meditatively.

The Father is not the Son, the Son is not the Holy Spirit, and the Holy Spirit is not the Father. If they are not, then who are they? Each personality is God expressing Himself in a distinct way for a specific purpose. In theology, this is called the Holy Trinity. Prayerfully the next sentence will help clear things up for you. The Father is God, the Son is God, and the Holy Spirit is God. There is only one God, who has chosen to express Himself through the Father, the Son, and the Holy Spirit. The tripersonality of God is incomprehensible to the finite human mind. I would be leery of anyone who makes the claim they do comprehend the Holy Trinity.

The Trinity can be expressed this way—the unity of the Father, Son, and Holy Spirit as three persons in one Godhead. Everything comes from the Father, through the Son, and in the Holy Spirit. Triunity is the state of being three in one—God over us (Father), God with us (Jesus), and God in us (Holy Spirit).

Now back to the fourth question we posed. Who is the Holy Spirit? Let's let Jesus answer this question for us. Before His death and resurrection from death and the grave, Jesus gave His disciples some startling news. He told them He was going away. Jesus had been *with* these handpicked men for three years. Hearing the news of His impending departure shook them to the core. To subdue their fears, Jesus made a promise to His disciples. When He went away, He would send *another* to be not only *with* them but more importantly, to live *in them*. This is so important for every believer to grasp that I feel the need to say it again. There are two words in the Greek language for another; one is *allos* (of like kind) and the other word is *heteros* (of different kind). Jesus uses the word allos when He said that He would send another, not just to be with them (like He had been), but to live in them. In His physical form, Jesus could not be with and in everyone at the same time, but the Holy Spirit can. The Holy Spirit residing in every believer is the presence of the indwelling Christ, for they are one. The Holy Spirit can be in all of his children at the same time. As a matter of fact, the Bible tells us that we are the temple of the Holy Spirit (1 Corinthians 6:19 NKJV). We are God's house.

If the Father is God and Jesus is God and they certainly claimed to be, then who is the Holy Spirit? I think the answer is obvious by now. The Holy Spirit has to be God. This is called the *triunity*—one God expressing Himself through three distinct personalities. What an incredible revelation. God resides in all of his children in the person of the Holy Spirit. The Holy Spirit is God's present to us, and his presence in us. Maybe it's time for us to breathe in some fresh air.

Public Meeting

In Acts 2 we have God fulfilling the promise He made to His disciples. The Holy Spirit had been with them, but the day was coming when the Holy Spirit would be in them. That day has come—Pentecost. "The Spirit of truth, whom the world cannot receive, because it neither sees Him nor knows Him; but you know Him, for He dwells with you and *will be in you*" (John 14:17 NKJV, emphasis added). In Acts 2, God is breathing Himself out in the person of the Holy Spirit on the 120 who had gathered together to wait for His power to fall. This is a public demonstration of the forever-abiding presence of God. "Nevertheless I tell you the truth.

It is to your advantage that I go away; for if I do not go away the Helper will not come to you; but if I depart, *I will send Him* [Holy Spirit] *to you*" (John 16:7 NKJV, emphasis added). The spirit of God goes from being with His followers to being in them. The same is true for all believers. The abiding presence of the Holy Spirit is what empowers and equips us to be His witnesses to the entire world. This was not a private meeting that took place during the nighttime like the disciples had with Jesus. This outpouring of the spirit took place during the daytime and was witnessed by a multitude of people.

There is an intriguing correlation between Genesis 2 and Acts 2 that I have never seen until recently. Both events involve the breath of God: God breathing out and making it possible for humanity to breathe in. Let's begin with the Genesis passage, then we will take a look at Acts 2. After we do, I think you will be able to see what connects these two events is the breath of God.

"At the time God made Earth and Heaven, before any grasses or shrubs had spouted from the ground—God hadn't yet sent rain on Earth, nor was there anyone around to work the ground (the whole Earth was watered by underground springs)—*God formed Man out of dirt from the ground and blew into his nostrils the breath of life. The Man came alive—a living soul*" (Genesis 2:7 TPT, emphasis added). What this verse says can easily be overlooked if we don't slow down our reading. I'm going to repeat what I've already said a few times already because we need to hear it again and again. The human body was formed by God from dirt. What was this body able to do before God breathed life into it? Not one thing. The physical body does not have the ability to know God, love God, obey God, or serve God. It takes the breath of God, and only the breath of God, to impart life to the lifeless. The declaration of Genesis 2 is clear. The man did not come alive (a living soul, a speaking spirit) until God blew His breath into his nostrils. The man could not do what he was created for until the spirit of God took up residence inside him. Without God's breath, there is no life. If God doesn't breathe out, we don't breathe in.

The first man was formed from the dust of the ground, giving him a physical (natural) body, but he did not possess life. Life comes from the spirit, not the flesh. For Adam to live, God had to impart life into him. And God did this by breathing Himself into Adam's body that He had formed from a physical substance—dirt. Once this happened, the man became a living soul, a speaking spirit.

Process this thought, the first house God lived in was a human house. This human house became contaminated in Genesis 3, and God had to move out. In Acts 2, God in the person of the Holy Spirit is moving back into human houses, and He will never leave.

In Acts 2, we see God taking up permanent residence in humankind by breathing His life into them. From this point on, God is not only with His children, He lives inside of them in the person of the Holy Spirit. Every person born into this world possesses natural life (physical) but not spiritual life until they have a born from above experience with the Lord Jesus Christ. This also makes it perfectly clear that our bodies are only earth suits for our spirits to live in. We are not physical beings who have spirits. We are spiritual beings who live in physical bodies. I like to call the human body a dirt suit where the new creation spirit of a child God lives. The spiritual is far more important than the natural. This is the reason Jesus told Nicodemus that He had to be born again, born from above. He already had a born-from-below (natural) experience, but physical life will not place a person in the right standing with God. It requires a second birth date.

In Acts 2, God is fulfilling the promise he made to his disciples in John 14:17. The spirit of God had been *with them*, but there was coming a time when the spirit of God would live *in them*. God will take up residence again in human-houses, and this time he will never move out. "And they were all filled with the Holy Spirit and began to speak with other tongues, as the Spirit gave them utterance" (Acts 2:4 NKJV).

The connecting link between Genesis 2 and Acts 2 is obvious. The breath of God is what imparts life. Maybe it's time for us to breathe in some fresh air.

EIGHT

Take a Deep Breath

The Spirit of God has made me, And the breath
of the Almighty gives me life.
—JOB 33:4 (NKJV)

S everal years ago, one of my old high school classmates called
to wish me a happy birthday. After making a few comments
about us being the same age as old people, he said, "Kniffen,
I have the answer to living a long life. All you have to do is follow
these instructions. Breathe in, breathe out—breathe in, breathe
out—breathe in, breathe out. You keep doing this, and I guarantee
you will live a long life." I never really liked this dude all that much.
All kidding aside, he is a great guy. There is one thing I will have to
concede. My friend is right. All we have to do is keep breathing to
live. Breathe in; breathe out.

There is a passage in the book of Acts that has become more and
more special to me over the years, especially in this final season of my
life on this side of eternity. "For in him [Jesus] we live and move and
exist. As some of your own poets have said, 'We are his offspring'"
(Acts 17:28 NLT). Once this verse becomes a living reality to you,

it makes it so much easier to slow down and turn a deaf ear to whatever is going on around you, and breathe deeply. Inhalation calms our spirits, and exhalation releases our fears. Sometimes the most effective thing we can do to promote our spiritual health is to stop and take a deep breath.

In December 1971 God gifted me with a precious and beautiful daughter. Melanie Jane Kniffen was born with an electric personality, charged with strong emotions. When she was growing up, there were times when everything was a crisis for her: friendships, boyfriends, school activities, whatever. You name it. Every event had the potential of becoming a flash point. When this happened, everything was as bad as it possibly could be. Believe it or not, this is actually a good personality trait when it is harnessed and expressed in a healthy way. And Melanie matured to the point where she was able to steward this supercharged personality she had been gifted with. Before she went to be with Jesus, she helped a lot of children as a speech pathologist.

God wired Melanie with this sensitive bent while she was being formed in the womb. You could say that her personality was supercharged. Any event could throw her into emotional overload when she was a teenager. My sweet girl could get hysterical. You never had to guess if she was upset about something. It was obvious and everyone knew it and I mean everyone. On occasions, you would have to sit her down and say, "Now, take a deep breath; relax, breathe slowly." Eventually she would get her emotions under control. Taking a deep breath was what made it possible for her to relax. Once she calmed down, she was able to get things in their proper perspectives. Sitting quietly and breathing deeply were how she was able to subdue the emotions that were holding her captive.

Life has a way of overloading us at times. Without warning, things can go into crisis mode. Panic takes over. Our emotions fly off the chart. If these feelings are not harnessed, it is possible for us to make decisions that may have serious consequences or do and say things that can cause a lot of pain to others and to ourselves. During these times our heavenly Father tells us to slow down, take a deep breath, relax, and breathe slowly. We breathe in the peace of God and exhale fear. Maybe my old friend from high school was right when he told me that if I want to live a long life, I need to breathe in, breathe out, breathe in, breathe out. You might give this a try yourself. A little practice won't hurt.

If everyone on this planet were to collaborate in writing books about all the things that have the ability to take the wind out of our emotional sails, the project would never be finished because the list is inexhaustible. What I want to do is deal with a few events that are shared by all of humanity, and have the tendency to knock the wind out of us. Take a deep breath, and let's get started.

Death of a Loved One

Separation caused by death can seem so final, oftentimes leaving a person bewildered and confused, even those who are strong in their faith. As I type this sentence, it has been one year since my incredible covenant partner went to be with Jesus. Like so many others, I know how hard it is to breathe when the sobering reality that your loved one will never be returning to this earthly realm smacks you in the face. It will literally take the breath out of you. Sermons and Bible lectures are not what a person needs during these heart-wrenching moments. People just need to be able to breathe.

The death of a loved one has a way of knocking the skids out from under us. We can prepare for death, but I don't think we are ever ready for it. Maybe there is some truth in what we have heard about the certainty of death. The only thing for sure in life is death and taxes. Grieving over the death of a loved one can be very debilitating, to say the least. Some days we do fairly well, and on other days, we crash and burn. This is a part of the healing process. Our ever-changing emotions can jerk us around like a kite on a string in high wind. If the string ever snaps, it's Katie bar the door. The lives of far too many children of God have been placed on hold because of spiritual respiratory complications. The pain of an event has left them with the inability to respire: to inhale and exhale the breath of God for the purpose of maintaining life. The emotional anguish that comes from being separated from a loved one by death has the ability to knock the wind out of our souls. At times it is difficult to relax, take a deep breath, and breathe slowly. But this is exactly what we must do when the pain of loss overwhelms us: breathe slowly while we set our mind and affections on things above. "Blessed are those who mourn, For they shall be comforted" (Matthew 5:4 NKJV).

Here is some exciting news. Believers are not immune from heartaches, tragedies, hurts, tribulations, and death while living on this earthly side of eternity. Well, maybe I overhyped the good news part. Being strong in faith does not exempt us from experiencing the hurts and pains that life can and will throw at us. To believe we can is to live our lives in self-deception. Deception is dangerous because it can be so deceiving. Yes, you read that right. It might be helpful to read it one more time before moving on.

Jesus said that as long as we live in this life (in this earthly realm), we will experience heartaches and grief just like those who are not believers (John 16:33 NKJV). It is not a matter of if we do, it's when. When we find ourselves going through uncertain times, there is one thing we can be certain about—our God is faithful, and He has given us His promise that He would walk with us through our grieving seasons. He is our hope and light. So the best thing we can do for ourselves when we suffer loss is to take a deep breath, relax, and breathe slowly. We must never forget that God is our breath.

Loneliness

Feelings of loneliness are just that—feelings. In no way am I discounting or denying the importance of feelings. Without feelings, humanity would only be mechanical robots, having a sensor system, a power supply, and a computer brain. On second thought, maybe humanity is closer to becoming that than we would like to admit. I'm just saying.

Feelings are real, but they may not be true. You can feel that God does not love you, but the truth is He is madly in love with you. He has always been and will always be. "For He Himself has said 'I will never leave you nor forsake you'" (Hebrews 13:5 NKJV). No matter what we find ourselves going through there is one constant, we can count on that God will never turn His heart from us, never. Knowing this truth helps us to relax and breathe slower and deeper.

Since feelings are real, they have the ability to convince us that what we are feeling is true. Always confront your feelings with the truth. Truth is whatever God says. When feelings of loneliness invade our emotional space, it makes it easy for us to throw a pity party and be the only invited guest. I've had a few of these in my lifetime. I never enjoyed the party either.

The enemy of our souls is very skilled at using loneliness to isolate us. He knows that if a person spends a prolonged amount of time disengaged, it will increase the chances of them becoming statistics. Many strong believers have succumbed to this devious scheme. In order to remain healthy in our thought lives, we must do whatever it takes not to allow this to happen. Whatever we do, we must never disconnect from our lifeline—our family of faith. The best way not to is to take a deep breath, relax, and breathe slowly. It seems like we have heard this before. Maybe just maybe it is the key to overcoming loneliness.

Extended periods of isolation increase the chances for a child of God to throw up their hands and surrender to their pain. It makes it easy for us to embrace the lie that life will never get any better. You will be by yourself for the rest of your life. That is a lie from the enemy of our souls. If he is successful in accomplishing his assignment (to kill, steal, and destroy), we become susceptible to all kinds of destructive emotions. Loneliness is one of the most effective tools the devil has in his arsenal. He is accomplished at using feelings of loneliness to keep us at the bottom of our emotional barrel.

I am going to share with you a good way to deal with loneliness. It is very simple, but you may find it to be the most difficult thing to do. Sit still at the feet of Jesus. Don't say a word. Sit, soak, and breathe deeply. No one, and I mean no one has ever experienced loneliness the way Jesus did. He knows how you feel but in greater depths. The people who said they would never desert Him did not honor their words. "But he [Peter] spoke more vehemently, 'If I have to die with You, I will not deny You!' And *they all* [disciples] *said likewise*" (Mark 14:31 NKJV, emphasis added). This would be a great testimony if these were the last words spoken by Peter and Jesus's disciples. But when push came to shove, they all forsook Him (Mark 14:50). He was left alone.

As you sit quietly at the feet of Jesus, you are sitting at the feet of someone who has empathy for how you feel. Do not say a word. Just sit still and set your mind and affection on him. If you sit quietly long enough, you will begin to experience His presence and His unending love for you. You will discover that you are not alone and never will be. Take a deep breath, relax, and breathe slowly.

Fear

Let me share with you a tidbit of information about what Jesus said about fear. Jesus never told anyone they should not feel fear. What He did say on many occasions was not to be afraid. Feeling fear and being afraid are not synonymous terms. God wants us to be filled with hope and trust, not fear. "Peace I leave with you, My peace I give to you; not as the world gives do I give to you. Let not your heart be troubled, *neither let it be afraid*" (John 14:27 NKJV, emphasis added).

When I was growing up, getting the wind knocked out of me was not uncommon. We were pretty rowdy kids, especially us boys. I think the medical expression is momentarily losing the ability to get air into our lungs. Whatever you call it does not change the fact that you cannot breathe when this happens. But it is not the air that has become your problem. It's your diaphragm. When you inhale, the diaphragm pulls down to help pull air into the lungs. When you exhale, the diaphragm pushes up to help push air out of the lungs. When this procedure is interfered with, no one has to tell you that you have a problem with breathing. Getting the breath knocked out of you is not life-threatening, but it can be terrifying.

A blow to the stomach or back can cause a spasm in your diaphragm. The muscle contracts, tenses up, and cannot do what it is designed to do and that is to help you breathe. If this ever happens to you, try to relax, go into a fetal position, and take slow, deep breaths through the nose. It won't be long before you begin to feel better: Take a deep breath, relax, and breathe slowly

Fear has the ability to affect our spiritual breathing as a punch in the stomach can do to our physical breathing. When it happens, you think you are not going to recover. It can lead to panic. Once in panic mode, no bad decisions are off-limits. It will not be long until feelings of hopelessness creep in, causing us to believe that we will never know peace again. This is why Jesus said on many occasions, "Be not afraid."

"For God has not given us *a spirit* of fear, but of power and of love and of a sound mind" (2 Timothy 1:7 NKJV, emphasis added). I have italicized *a spirit* because I want you to see that fear is *a spirit* and not just a feeling. Fear is a demonic spirit that Satan uses in an attempt to knock the breath of God out of our spiritual lives. This is something he succeeds in doing more often than he fails. When a life experience hits us hard, we need to remain calm and continue to take deep breaths. It will not be long before peace will overtake the fear that has assaulted us.

When I first entered the ministry, I heard a statement that I filed away in my memory bank. After many years of ministry under my belt, I understand how true it is. Fear and faith have something in common. Both believe something is going to happen. Fear tries to convince us it will be bad, and faith believes it will be good. Since we have been given free will, we can choose which one we embrace— good or bad. I vote that we sit still, be quiet, and go with faith.

Hopelessness

Nothing is more debilitating than feelings of hopelessness. Losing all hope or nearly all robs us of any expectations of things ever getting better. Thoughts like *I have no future, no one understands how I feel, I might as well give up, it is too late now, all hope is gone,* or *I will never be happy again* become constant companions. Sometimes a person chooses to deal with temporary problems in a permanent way by taking their own lives.

Hopelessness is a common experience of patients with depressive disorder (DD) and an important predictor of suicidal behavior. This is the ultimate goal of our enemy. His job description is found in the Gospel of John. "The thief [devil] does not come except to steal, and to kill, and to destroy" (John 10:10 NKJV, emphasis added). Among the worst demons of peace are fear and loneliness. To lose all expectations of things ever getting better can wreck a person for life. "Hope [confident expectation] deferred [postponed, delayed] makes the heart sick, But *when* the desire comes, it is a tree of life" (Proverbs 13:12 NKJV emphasis). It is so easy for us to overlook something that this verse says because we are so focused on the first part of it. It says *when* the desire comes, not if hope comes but when. I love The Passion Translation of this verse. "When hope's dream seems to drag on and on, the delay can be depressing. But when at last your dream comes true, life's sweetness will satisfy your soul" (Proverbs 13:12 TPT). Whatever you are going through or will ever go through, whatever storm you are facing, joy is yours when you place your hope in Jesus. "We have this certain hope like a strong, unbreakable anchor holding our souls to God himself. Our anchor of hope is fastened to the mercy seat in the heavenly realm beyond the sacred threshold" (Hebrews 6:19 TPT). Our anchor holds in spite of the severity of the storms that we will face in our lives.

"The Anchor Holds" is a song sung by Ray Boltz that has ministered to an untold number of people since its release in 1995. The song is about how the storms of life can beat us down. But no matter how fierce the storms may be, it is just like the song, "The Anchor Holds."

> The anchor holds
> Though the ship is battered
> The anchor holds
> Though the sails are torn
>
> I have fallen on my knees
> As I faced the raging seas
> The anchor holds
> In spite of the storm

The words of this song could be the testimony of every one of us. The best place to stand when the storms of life hit is on our knees. No matter how intense the storm may be, our anchor holds.

If a spirit of hopelessness ever gets its tentacles wrapped around our emotions, we become more susceptible to nose-diving into the pit of depression. The depression pit can be very confining too. The way out, you guessed it, is to relax, take a deep breath, and breathe slowly. If you do not remember anything else by the time you finish reading this book, I pray you will never forget what I have said many times—God is our breath. "For *in him* we live and move and have our being" (Acts 17:28 NKJV, emphasis added). As long as our heavenly Father keeps breathing out, we will be able to breathe in.

Emotional Hurts

There is no way to get through life without being scathed by emotional hurts. It is not going to happen. Sometimes the pain and hurts are inflicted on us by the actions or words of people. Oftentimes emotional hurt is the result of grief or loss. It really does not matter what caused it. Emotional pain is real, and it can be intense at times. Left unabated, it can cause issues in other areas of our lives, and that includes our physical health.

If we do not stay on our toes, feelings can congeal to the point where we become bosom *buddies* with persistent pain. All it takes for emotional pain to resurface is a triggering event. These events can be memories, words, actions, smells, sounds—the list is inexhaustible. In other words, triggers can be internal, external, or sensory.

As we said earlier, acute emotional pain can lead to physical harm. God's Word tells us this, "Dear friend, I hope all is well with you and that you are as *healthy in body* as you are *strong in spirit*" (3 John 1:21 NLT, emphasis added). If we are not emotionally healthy, it can lead to physical complications.

No matter how hopeless you may feel, life goes on even when you don't want it to. Carrying emotional pain into our tomorrow becomes our choice. "Therefore strengthen the hands which hang down, and the feeble knees, and make straight paths for your feet so that what is lame may not be dislocated, *but rather be healed*" (Hebrews 12:12–14 NKJV, emphasis added). Do not allow unhealthy thoughts to enter your emotional space with impunity. Judge them and the ones that you do not recognize the holiness of God in and cast them out as quickly as possible. Whatever you do, do not procrastinate. The longer you hold on to them, the more they will control you.

We need to be good stewards of the healing God has breathed into us. God helps us so we can help others. We are surrounded by hurting people. God wants to breathe His healing breath through us on someone who is downcast and may be contemplating surrendering to the enemy's bluffs. One timely word may be the very thing God uses to keep them vertical. "Do to others whatever you would like them to do to you. This is the essence of all that is taught in the law and the prophets" (Matthew 7:12 NLT).

Let me share something with you that you may have never heard or thought about. When your emotions seem to be running away with you and when life seems like it is imploding, take a deep breath, relax, and breathe slowly. On second thought, maybe you have heard this.

NINE

This Is the Air I Breathe

> If God were to take back his spirit and withdraw his breath, all
> life would cease, and humanity would turn again to dust.
> —JOB 34:14–15 (NLT)

I think most of us know what will happen if we unplug a running fan from its power source. It loses its ability to operate. The moment you unplug a fan, it stops running. Electricity is what gives the fan the power to function properly. If there is no power source, there's no life.

What is true about a fan is even more true regarding our lives. Without the breath of God, all life ceases. Humanity will return to dust. All life is dependent on the breath of God for its existence. He is the air we breathe.

On September 11, 2001, Michael W. Smith released a song called "This Is the Air I Breathe" under the label of Reunion Records. The lyrics of this song remind us that our very existence is dependent on the Lord Jesus Christ. We cannot exist without the breath of God sustaining our physical bodies and the breath of God sustaining our souls and spirits. Without Him, it is impossible for us to breathe.

This is the air I breathe
This is the air I breathe
Your holy presence living in me

This is my daily bread
This is my daily bread
Your very word spoken to me

And I I'm desperate for you
And I I'm lost without you

God's grace is what keeps Him from taking back His spirit and withdrawing His breath from us. Without Him, there is no life. "For you died to this life, and your real life is hidden with Christ in God. And when Christ, *who is your life*, is revealed to the whole world, you will share in all his glory" (Colossians 3:3–4 NLT, emphasis added). He is the air we breathe. God's breath is His holy presence living in us.

This would be a good time to revisit the moment in the book of Genesis when God created humankind. "And the Lord God formed man of the dust of the ground and *breathed into his nostrils the breath of life*; and *man became a living being*" (Genesis 2:7 NKJV, emphasis added). A man became a living soul, literally a speaking spirit. What was he before God breathed air into him? What was he able to do? The answer is not one thing. Without God breathing into humankind, there is no life. He was nothing more than particles of dust—there was no life to be found in Adam until God imparted His life into him by His breath. If God never breathed out, we would never breathe in. He is the air we breathe.

Try to picture in your mind the scene that Genesis 2:7 describes. Here is a dirt suit that God had formed out of the dust of the ground. This suit of clay had no life in it, rendering it lifeless. There is no animation whatsoever in this lump of soil. Lying there without moving, communicating, thinking, feeling, or talking was all it could do because the body was only an empty shell without the breath of God living on the inside of it. The only thing this earth suit could do was lie there.

After God imparted life to Adam, we find him talking, giving animals their names, and tending God's garden. He is now alive because he is carrying the spirit of God inside him. Maybe Adam was the first person to release the song "This Is the Air I Breath" and not Michael W. Smith. It's just a thought.

In the scriptures, the breath of God is more than the physical exchange of air in and out of the lungs. Breath in both the Greek and Hebrew languages is equated with God's spirit. It is a symbol of the life of God. That means that we are not physical beings who have a spirit. We are spiritual beings living inside physical bodies. The body has no life apart from the residing presence of the spirit of God. When God breathes, He is imparting His life. He is the air we breathe.

God's Breath Is Discernable

I live in a small town in the Panhandle of Texas that is known for the number of cattle it has in feed yards on any given month. When you enter the city limits, you will be greeted by a big sign that says, Beef Capital of the World. There are hundreds of feed yards in this part of the state of varying sizes. Eighty-eight percent of all cattle are fed in the Texas Panhandle. That's close to 2.5 million head. We have the highest density of beef feedlots in the region. There is one not too far from my home that has the capacity to feed more than 100,000 head of cattle at one time. It is usually full of beef on the hoof. That is a big feedlot! This is one place I usually take people who are visiting our area for the first time. People are overwhelmed with unbelief when they see so many cattle gathered in one place. It amazes me too, and I have lived here for years.

These cattle are being prepared for public consumption. This process is done by making sure the cattle have nutritious feed and clean water. The health of these bovines is a priority for all the feed yards. There are several meat processing plants in our region as well. I have personally been inside many of these plants and have witnessed firsthand the process the cattle go through from the feed yard to the BBQ grill from the feed trough in the feedlot to the plate on our tables. It is a fascinating thing to see.

I love to see the look on the faces of first-time visitors to our community who have never smelled a feed yard. "What is that smell?" This is usually the first thing a visitor says as they wrinkle their noises and make facial expressions of disgust. We usually answer their question with one word, "Money, that is the smell of money." The smell that a feed yard emits is enhanced after it rains. We do not get that much rain here in the Texas Panhandle, but when we do, hello, feed yards! Even the indigenous folks will cut up a little.

I have lived here long enough, so the smell does not bother me that much. When people ask me how to get to Hereford, Texas, I tell them to go west until they smell it and then head south until they step in it.

I think you understand the point I am trying to make by using the smell of feed yards to illustrate discerning the presence of God. The smell of a feed yard will get your undivided attention. When the breeze is just right, you will have no doubt there is a feed yard within rock-throwing distance. The smell of God's presence is just as detectable. How can it not be since He lives on the inside of us? How close is that? "Have you forgotten that your body is now the sacred temple of the Spirit of Holiness, who lives in you? You don't belong to yourself any longer, for the gift of God, the Holy Spirit, lives inside your sanctuary" (1 Corinthians 6:19 TPT). God's manifested presence is intoxicating. Once you get a scent of it, you will know He is near. No one will have to tell you that He is close by.

My Own Personal Experience

I'm not one who buys into things too quickly. You might say I'm a little slow. I have missed out on some good things because of my slowness to accept something, but it has also kept me from falling for things that turned out to have no merit. Human tendency is to judge things based on experience. If it is not our experience, then we are suspect of anyone who claims they have. And so it is with detecting the presence of God by His intoxicating breath. I have been told by many God-loving people that once you smell His presence, you will never forget it. I never doubted the sincerity of these people, but it was hard for me to wrap my mind around what they were saying because I had never had that experience. I have had thousands of experiences knowing and feeling the presence of God. But smelling His breath, to me that was in another orbit. Little did I know that I was in for a divine setup.

My search began. The burning desire within my soul was to know what the breath of God smells like if it can be smelled. Early on in my pursuit, I was amazed at how many scriptures there are that talk about the fragrance of God. His presence emits a smell that is unique and very calming. It is one of those moments when you know what is going on, but it is impossible to explain. When you share your experience with people, you are probably going to get one of those looks and this statement, "Sure you did."

God also has the ability to smell. By the way, His favorite scent is sacrifice. As new-creation beings in Christ, we have the ability to smell His presence because we are in Him, and He is in us (John 14:20 NKJV). You cannot be that intertwined with someone and not have the ability to smell them. What Paul said in his second letter to the church at Corinth was what the spirit of God used to create a desire deep within me to have a personal experience in this realm. "Our lives are a Christ-like fragrance rising up to God. But this fragrance is perceived differently by those who are being saved and by those who are perishing" (2 Corinthians 2:15 NLT). After meditating on this verse, I began a deliberation with myself. If God can smell us and we bear His divine nature (2 Peter 1:4), then we should be able to smell Him.

Did you know that there are some breeds of dogs that have an olfactory system that enables them to smell something twelve miles away? That is beyond human comprehension. Twelve miles, that is mind-blowing! If a dog can smell something twelve miles away, can you imagine how far God can smell? Let me give you a little insight. Since God is eternal, there are no limitations to His spiritual olfactory system. There is nothing out of His range of smell.

I placed this pursuit of smelling the presence of God on the back burner for a while. I never totally forgot about it, but I was OK with my lack of experience in this realm. Then it happened. In the middle of the night, I woke up to the presence of a smell I had never smelled before. It was incredible and indescribable. I have never smelled anything like it before. All of a sudden, I knew that I was smelling the presence of my heavenly Father. I was overcome by a peace and calmness I had never experienced before. No one had to tell me what had happened.

The next morning, I could not wait to tell my sweet wife about my nighttime encounter. She listened intently as I shared my experience. After I had finished, she smiled and said, "The smell of God is amazing, isn't it? I love to smell His presence." I had to give her an amen!

Men's Mountain Retreat

For many years I and several pastor friends of mine attended a men's retreat in the mountains of New Mexico. It was a three-day meeting that was filled with special moments. Everything about this conference was enjoyable. The praise and worship were off the charts. The messages delivered by the speakers were always a timely word. The facilities were excellent, and I might add, so was the food. We could not ask for a better men's conference to attend.

Before each session began, men would gather in the auditorium for a time of prayer. Some would walk back and forth in front of the stage as they prayed; others would sit quietly bathing the atmosphere with prayer. The leadership team of this conference placed great emphasis on prayer.

There was one man who was in charge of these prayer sessions. He would walk to one end of the stage and then back as he prayed out loud. This time of prayer would last thirty to forty-five minutes. When it was time for the meeting to begin, we could sense the presence of the Holy Spirit.

During one of these sessions, the prayer had reached a high pitch. I was sitting on the second row from the front of the auditorium with all my pastor friends—praying. All of a sudden, there was a fragrance, an aroma that every man in that row caught a whiff of at the same time. No one said a word, but we all looked at each other in silence knowing we were encountering the presence of God. His smell is undeniable.

No one said a word about what had happened until after the meeting was over. We all knew what an incredible moment we all had shared together. What is so amazing about this is no other row had this experience. You can imagine the conversation we had on our five-hour drive back home. Not one man questioned that we had a tangible manifestation of God's presence.

No one has to tell us when God breathes on us. We may not be able to articulate what we know, but we know. People may ask, "How do you know?" All we can say is "I just know." We are smelling the presence of God, and it is so calming. Let me say it again so you do not forget. The smell of God's breath makes it evident that He is close by. He is the air we breathe.

God's Favorite Smell

There are certain smells that always catch my attention. It is easy for me to recognize where they are coming from. I love the smell of fresh-cut grass, especially after a small rain shower. The smell of a horse has always been one of my favorites. But at the top of the list is the smell of leather. There is just something about this smell that I cannot resist. I could spend days in a saddle shop enjoying the aroma of all the horse tack. Most of the time I keep a buckskin candle burning in my home. The aroma it emits has a way of throttling me down. Everyone has their favorite smell as does God.

The aroma that will always get God's attention is the smell of sacrifices. That's right. A sacrifice has a recognizable smell to the nostrils of God. "Then Noah built an altar to the Lord, and took of every clean animal and of every clean bird, and offered burnt offerings on the altar. And *the Lord smelled a soothing aroma.* Then the Lord said in His heart, 'I will never again curse the ground for man's sake, although the imagination of man's heart is evil from his youth; nor will I again destroy every living thing as I have done'" (Genesis 8:20–21 NKJV, emphasis added). God smelled the sacrifices Noah offered on the altar he built after the flood had destroyed the earth and everything living in it. Sacrifices are God's favorite smell.

We do not offer sacrifices on altars today because Jesus is now our altar. He is our everything. As I have already said if God does not breathe out, we do not breathe in. There is no life without Him. "For in Him [Christ] we live and move and have our being, as also some of your own poets have said, 'For we are also His offspring'" (Acts 17: 28 NKJV). It does not sound like we can do much of anything apart from Him. Could it be that He is the air we breathe? There I said it again.

Even though we do not offer animal sacrifices today, there are still sacrifices to be made. Our willingness to sacrifice is how we demonstrate our devotion to God. Here is what Paul said to the church in Rome about presenting ourselves to God as a sacrifice. "I beseech you therefore, brethren, by the mercies of God, that you *present your bodies a living sacrifice,* holy, acceptable to God, which is your reasonable service" (Romans 12:1 NKJV, emphasis added). Did you notice that Paul said we are to present ourselves as living sacrifices? What is the difference between a dead sacrifice and a living sacrifice? Unlike a dead sacrifice, a living sacrifice has free will. It can crawl off the altar anytime it wills to. The desire of God is for us to offer ourselves wholeheartedly, living for Him with our entire being because of our love for Him.

I want to zero in on one of the many sacrifices the Word of God talks about—it is the sacrifice of praise. "*Therefore by Him let us continually offer the sacrifice of praise to God*, that is, the fruit of our lips, giving thanks to His name. But do not forget to do good and to share for with such sacrifices God is well pleased" (Hebrews 13:15–16 NKJV, emphasis added). We should always be willing to do good deeds and to share with others. The sacrifice of living a good quality life and blessing others pleases God. This is an aroma that attracts His presence every time. But doing good things comes after the sacrifice of praise is offered. If we get the first part right, there will be no hesitation whatsoever in doing good things, including sharing with others.

Why would Paul say that praise is a sacrifice? It seems like praise and sacrifice are mutually exclusive. At first glance, they seem to be incompatible. It is like tossing a coin and getting heads and tails at the same time. At first glance, it does not make sense.

A quick glance at a verse in the book of 1 Thessalonians will give us more insight into how praise can be a sacrifice. "*In everything give thanks; for this is the will of God in Christ Jesus for you*" (1 Thessalonians 5:18 NKJV, emphasis added). This verse does not say that we are to give thanks to God *for all things*. It says we are to give thanks *in all things*. It is easy to praise the Lord when the sun is shining, and everything is bright and clear. It is not hard to praise Him when things are going well. That is not a sacrifice. Praise becomes a sacrifice when things are dark and dreary. In the midst of everything, no matter how difficult it may be, we give praise to God with all of our hearts and souls. Praise is not lip service. It comes out of the deep secret places of our innermost beings, especially when life has thrown us a curve ball. What does a person do when they do the right things, pull the right levers, push the right buttons, and life caves in on them? They praise God anyway. This is why praise is called a sacrifice.

It is not difficult to praise God when everything seems to be going our way, but life can have sudden swings. Life is full of stormy days. It is in the turbulent moments of our lives where praise becomes a sacrifice. "I will praise the Lord at *all times*; His praise shall continually be in my mouth" (Psalm 34:1 NKJV, emphasis added).

When Jesus Breathed His Last

"And when Jesus had cried out with a loud voice, He said, 'Father, into Your hands I commit my Spirit.' Having said this, *He breathed His last*" (Luke 23:46 NKJV, emphasis added). Jesus breathed out His last breath on the cross so humanity could breathe in their first. Breath is life. Without it, there is no hope for humanity.

Let me end this chapter with two verses that have already been cited; one is from the Old Testament, and the other one is from the New Testament. "If God were to take back his spirit and withdraw his breath, all life would cease, and humanity would turn again to dust" (Job 34:14–15 NLT).

"For you died to this life, and your real life is hidden with Christ in God. And when Christ, who is your life, is revealed to the whole world, you will share in all his glory" (Colossians 3:3–4 NLT). Jesus is the air we breathe.

TEN

"Dem Bones Dem Bones"

So I spoke this message, just as he told me. Suddenly as I spoke, there
was a rattling noise all across the valley. The bones of each body
came together and attached themselves as complete skeletons.
—EZEKIEL 37:7 (NLT)

B ack in 1928, James Weldon Johnson wrote a song called
"Dem Bones Dem Bones." Some versions of this song are
credited to James's brother J. Rosamond Johnson. It is also
called the "Dry Bones" song. The famous Myers Jubilee Singers
recorded it the same year it was written and the rest is history.

As this song became more and more popular, it was used primarily
to help children learn the internal framework of the human body
called the skeleton. This song was the first anatomy lesson for small
children. It begins with the toe bone being connected to the foot
bone, the foot bone connected to the ankle bone, and the ankle bone
connected to the leg bone. From there, the song works its way up
the body's skeleton to the head bone, and then it works its way back
down to the toe bone. I still remember the lyrics to "Dem Bones"
after all these years. There are some things we just don't forget.

Even though many people can sing this cute "Dry Bones" song, only a few know where the inspiration came from for its writing. It was taken from the Bible. That's right, from the Word of God. Ezekiel 37:1–14 inspired James Weldon Johnson to write this incredible little song. This is why at the end of every section of the lyrics, we find these words, "Now hear the words of the Lord." Maybe we should give the prophet Ezekiel some credit for inspiring this song.

Valley of Dem Dry Bones

The spirit of the Lord carried Ezekiel away to a valley filled with scattered bones. This is clearly a prophetic vision that God gave the prophet Ezekiel that has both a historical and spiritual setting. Historically it is a picture of God's people who had been driven from their homeland and scattered throughout the known world. They felt their nation was finished and would never be revived.

Spiritually this vision depicts the disconnection from God caused by rebellion and unbelief. When someone chooses to do life without God and is disobedient to His word, it is only a matter of time before their lives become scattered and disconnected from their life source. This is the dead waiting to die.

As far as Ezekiel could see, there were skeletal remains littered across the valley floor separated and completely dried out. There was no sign of life anywhere. It was a valley of the shadow of death. As Ezekiel looked over this huge depression of the earth's surface, he was overcome with disbelief and despair. In the midst of his shock, God spoke to him. "Then he asked me, 'Son of man, can these bones become living people again'" (Ezekiel 37:3 NLT). I am sure Ezekiel's first thought was what ours probably would have been—ain't no way! We may not know what Ezekiel actually thought, but we do know what he said in response to God's question, "'O Sovereign Lord,' I replied, '*you alone know* the answer to that'" (Ezekiel 37:3 NLT, emphasis added). From man's perspective, this is a hopeless situation. But we need to remember that with God, all things are possible, even imparting life into dry disarticulated bones.

Ezekiel spoke exactly what God told him to say to the lifeless bones. This reveals a very important biblical truth that must not be overlooked. The breath of God is the only power that can impart life: to bring hope to a hopeless situation. To see this, all we have to do is go back to the first two chapters of the book of Genesis. All things came into existence by the spoken Word of God. Life is in God's breath. Only His breath can give life, and the only thing that can sustain life is His breath. Without God breathing out, nothing will ever be able to breathe in.

In case you missed it, I will repeat something I said earlier. The words Ezekiel spoke were not his own. This is very important for us to understand. God did not give Ezekiel the freedom to say whatever he wanted to say to the dry scattered bones. God told him exactly what to say. What we have is God speaking to the dry bones (Israelites) through the mouth of Ezekiel. These separated and disjointed bones began to come together, not by what the prophet said but by what God said to these dry bones through the prophet Ezekiel. This is crucial to our understanding of where life comes from. The breath of God is His Word. There is no life apart from it.

We must never forget that our tongues have the ability to speak life or death. "Life and death are in the power of the tongue, And those who love it will eat its fruit" (Proverbs 18:21 NKJV). Since God has given us free will, we have a choice of what comes out of our mouths—life or death. In case you are wavering about which one to choose, I suggest you speak life. I'm just saying.

Dem Bones Began to Rattle

What we see unfolding in Ezekiel 37 is the same thing that took place in Genesis 1. "The earth was formless and empty, and darkness covered the deep waters. And the Spirit of God was hovering [brooding] over the surface of the waters" (Genesis 1:2 NLT). In verse 3, God begins to speak, "Then God said, 'Let there be light,' and there was light" (Genesis 1:3 NLT). My version of this verse would be something like this, "Then God began to breathe and life began to spring up." The breath of God is life.

When God speaks, He is releasing His breath, and when He does, the impossible becomes a reality. "So I spoke this message, just as he told me. Suddenly as I spoke, there was a rattling noise all across the valley. The bones came together and attached themselves as complete skeletons" (Ezekiel 37:7 NLT). Since God's breath is the source of all life, dem dry bones Ezekiel saw covering the valley floor had no choice but to come alive. When God breathes, the lifeless hears and they have to respond.

The sound of rattling coming from the valley floor alerts us that something is happening. God is taking life out of death. "Then as I watched, muscles and flesh formed over the bones. Then skin formed to cover their bodies, but they still had no breath in them. Then he said to me, Speak a prophetic message and say, This is what the Sovereign Lord says: Come, O breath, from the four winds! Breathe into these dead bodies so they may live again. So I spoke the message as he commanded me, and breath came into their bodies. They all came to life and stood up on their feet—a great army" (Ezekiel 37:8–10 NLT).

What a sight this must have been. Dry bones went from being separated and scattered to complete and whole when the breath of God was spoken over them. When God speaks, He brings life to the lifeless and hope to the hopeless. His breath will change any environment. There is nothing that will not respond to His voice, *nothing!*

God made the following promise to the Israelites, "Then he said to me, 'Speak a prophetic message to these bones and say, Dry bones, listen to the word of the Lord'! This is what the Sovereign Lord says: 'Look! I am going to put breath into you and make you live again! I will put flesh and muscles on you and cover you with skin. I will put breath into you, and you will come to life. Then you will know that I am the Lord'" (Ezekiel 37:4–6 NLT). The phrase "listen to the word of the Lord" found in verse 4 is in James Weldon Johnson's song "Dem Bones Dem Bones." I can almost hear the entire valley of dried-bones choir singing in harmony to this song of life. There is a good possibility that the clattering we are hearing today is more than just noise.

Maybe it is time for us to start listening for the rattling Ezekiel heard. I am convinced that we are living in a day when God is bringing to life what so many of us thought was forever dead. There's a shaking in the family of faith. There is a movement of the spirit of God in many of our public schools, there is an awakening within our communities, there is hope arising in many regions in our country and around the world, and there is a rattling sound coming forth that cannot be quenched or ignored any longer. The breath of God is blowing, and life is springing up in places where we believed all hope was gone.

God's Word Is the Spirit and Life

Sometimes life will knock the breath out of us. There is not a person on this planet who is immune or exempt from having this happen to them in the course of living life in this earthly realm. It goes with the territory of being a part of humanity. Jesus even told us that as long as we are in this world, we will have some challenging seasons but to rejoice because He has overcome the world. When hurtful life events suck the wind out of us, we find ourselves in need of some motivational oomph. And we can only get this lift from the breath of God, His word. "The Spirit alone gives eternal life. Human effort accomplishes nothing. And the very words I have spoken to you are *spirit* and *life*" (John 6:63 NLT, emphasis added).

"Lazarus, come forth"—Jesus spoke these words to the four-day resident of a sealed tomb. He was the brother of Mary and Martha.

John recorded this story in chapter 11 of his Gospel account. This chapter would be a great passage for personal Bible reading and study. To know that God can bring all of our dead and buried dreams back to life again causes hope and expectancy to arise in our spirits. All we need is for Him to speak. His breath is the spirit and life.

When Jesus called Lazarus out of the tomb, it was to show Mary and Martha, along with all of their grieving friends, that physical death is not what most people think it is. "And whoever believes in Me *shall never die*" (John 11:26 NKJV, emphasis added). Don't allow these words to pass through one ear and out of the other. What did Jesus say? He said that if we believe in Him, we will *never* die. I wonder what never means. Do you think it really means never? Keep this in mind, Jesus was one who meant what He said and said what He meant.

After the stone was removed from the entrance of the tomb, Jesus said, "Lazarus, come forth" (John 11:43 NKJV)! In response to Jesus's words (breath) "Lazarus come forth," the one who everyone thought was gone forever obeyed and came out of the tomb. "And he who had died came out bound hand and foot with graveclothes, and his face was wrapped with a cloth. Jesus said to them, 'Loose him, and let him go'" (John 11:44 NKJV). It is so easy to get caught up in this story that we do exactly what I warned us not to do. In case you have already forgotten, I will remind you. Jesus said, "And *whoever believes in Me shall never die*" (John 11:26 NKJV, emphasis added). This begs the question did Jesus call Lazarus out of the grave to give him life or to show his sisters and friends that he was still alive? As you make your decision, keep in mind what Jesus told Martha.

We have a similar story in chapter 5 of Mark's Gospel. A synagogue official named Jairus had a twelve-year-old daughter who was at the point of death. In desperation, he came and fell at the feet of Jesus and begged Him to come to heal his daughter. During a short delay, a report came to Jairus that his daughter had died. Jesus said something to this father that seemed so callous. He told Jairus to keep believing. How in the world could he keep believing when the report he received about his daughter was so grim? But that was exactly what Jesus told him. Could it be that Jesus knew something about death that most of us didn't?

When Jesus, Peter, James, and John got to Jairus's house, they found it surrounded by a large crowd of grieving friends and neighbors. There was loud wailing and moaning echoing throughout the neighborhood. Jesus said something that changed the atmosphere from grieving to mocking and ridicule. He said, "Why make this commotion and weep? The child is not dead, but sleeping" (Mark 5:39 NKJV). Jesus sent everyone outside, except for His disciples and the little girl's mother and father. Once everyone was removed from the house, Jesus took the little girl by the hand and said, "Talitha, cumi," which is translated, Little girl, I say to you, arise. Immediately the girl arose and walked, for she was twelve years of age. "And they were overcome with great amazement" (Mark 5:41–42).

Let me repeat something that I have said twice already because it can slip past us without us realizing it. Jesus said, "Whoever believes in me shall never die." This is mind-blowing. Death has no life for a child of God. We will never die? How can that be? When Jesus died on the cross, life was taken out of death for those who had placed their trust in Him. Death was no match for the last breath Jesus breathed on the cross. He breathed out so we could breathe in. God's Word is the spirit and life.

Speak to Your Dry Bones

Have you ever thought about having or had a memorial service for some of your dreams? Have you ever felt like the vision you had for your life ended up in the dumpster? Have you ever lost hope, believing things will never get better? Have you ever felt like life is passing you by? When hope is deferred, the human tendency is to shift into survival mode. Thriving is no longer on the radar screen, surviving is. Until we are promoted to the sweet by-and-by we will have to struggle in order to survive in the nasty now-and-now. This is not the life God intends for His children to live.

Let me go on record. In life, there are more bills than thrills. It's not always moonlight and roses; most of the time it's daylight and dishes. Sometimes we don't find in life what we expected, and we didn't expect what we found. Welcome to life.

No matter what we may face in this unpredictable earthly realm, the battles we find ourselves engaged in and the raging storms that are trying to pull us under, Jesus is our rock and our anchor. He is the only one who can bring stability to our lives in the midst of a storm. Ray Boltz's song "The Anchor Holds" echoes this truth:

> I have fallen on my knees
> As I faced the raging seas
> The anchor holds
> In spite of the storm

"This hope we have as an anchor of the soul, both sure and steadfast and which enters the Presence behind the veil, where the forerunner has entered for us, even Jesus, having become High Priest forever according to the order of Melchizedek" (Hebrews 6:19–20 NKJV). No matter how severe the storms we face may be or how out of control things appear, Jesus is our anchor that holds. He is our hope.

When God brought Ezekiel out in the spirit and set his feet in a valley surrounded by dry bones, he did not have an iPhone to take pictures of this gruesome scene to post on Facebook. I wish he had because they say a picture is worth a thousand words. We may have to use our imaginations to get an idea of how devastating this scene was, but there is one thing we do know for certain—God always has the last word about everything. When He speaks, even dry bones hear Him and obey. Ask Lazarus and Jairus's daughter.

What Ezekiel said to the dry bones that littered the valley were not his own. God told him what to say, and to his credit, he was obedient. Life was restored by the breath of God, not from what the prophet had to say. This provides us with insight into how we are to speak to our valleys of dry bones. We simply say what God says. In the book of Proverbs, we are told that both death and life are in our mouths. Life is in what God says, and death is in what fallen humanity says (Proverbs 18:21 NKJV). We need to breathe His Words over every situation that tries to keep us from living our new creation lives. We do this by speaking His Word (His Word is His breath) over whatever is going on in our lives. As the song says, "I Speak Jesus" (Charity Gayle).

What valley do you find yourself in right now? Does your situation look hopeless? Have the dreams and visions you had for your life died? Is there the smell of death in any part of your life? Here's some good news. Death can actually be the soil that real hope springs up in. God is still in the business of taking life out of death. He does this with His breath (Word). When God breathes out, we are able to breathe in. The smell of God's breath is undeniable.

KniffKnotes Paraphrase of Ezekiel 37:5–10

I'm going to end this chapter with my own personal paraphrase of Ezekiel 37:5–10. I call it the KniffKnotes paraphrase. Keep in mind the spiritual setting of this passage, not the historical record as you read this. God is talking to the Israelites through His prophet, but He is also talking to you and me. What I want you to see is that our lives come from and are sustained by the breath of God living on the inside of us. Without His life dwelling in us, we are nothing more than dry bones. Now hear the word of the Lord.

The Lord is speaking to the valley of scattered dry bones through His prophet Ezekiel. "Bones, I am going to breathe My breath into you, and you will live again. I will put you back together better than you were before. My breath will be in you, and you shall live. And when this happens, you will know that I am who I say I am—I am the Lord."

When these words were spoken, a rattling sound could be heard all over the valley floor. The scattered bones were restored to their proper places just like God said they would. The bones of each individual came back together as they should be. But something was missing. Even though they were whole again, there was no breath in them, kind of like the body of the first Adam. The body was complete, but there was no life present until God breathed His life into it. This was when humanity became a living soul, a speaking spirit. God told Ezekiel to prophesy to the breath. "Breath, hear what the Lord has to say. Come from all directions, north, south, east, and west. Breathe on these dry bones." Ezekiel was obedient and said exactly what God told him to say. And all of a sudden, every individual stood up on their feet. They looked like an exceedingly great army. What was dead is living again. The Lord took the life out of death.

Life is in the Word of God. "It is the Spirit who gives life; the flesh profits nothing. The words I speak to you are spirit, and they are life" (John 6:63 NKJV). When we are reading the written Word of God, we are literally smelling the breath of God. They are inseparable. "In the beginning was the Word, and the Word was with God, and the Word was God" (John 1:1 NKJV).

No matter what situation you may find yourself in, do as the song says, "I Speak Jesus."

'Cause Your name is power
Your name is healing
Your name is life
Break every stronghold
Shine through the shadows
Burn like a fire

Thank you, Jesse Reeves, Dustin Smith, Abby Benton, Kristen Dutton, Carlene Prince, Raina Pratt, and Charity Gayle for an incredible song.

ELEVEN

The Smell of God's Presence

> Now thanks be to God who always leads us in triumph in Christ, and through us diffuses the fragrance of His knowledge in every place. For we are to God the fragrance of Christ among those who are being saved and among those who are perishing. To the one we are the aroma of death leading to death, and to the other the aroma of life leading to life.
> —2 CORINTHIANS 2:14-16 (NLT)

A man with poor hygiene walked into a crowded elevator. The odor he was emitting was bad, really, really bad. Once the door of the elevator shut, there was no way for the odor to escape, making the situation even worse. Everyone on board was held captive by the stench. People were holding their noses and elbowing each other as they pointed to the man who had just gotten on the elevator. Everyone wanted to say something but didn't want to offend or embarrass the man. Finally someone worked up the courage and said, "Oh my, someone's deodorant is failing them." The man with poor hygiene said, "Don't look at me. I don't use it."

We Carry the Smell of God

Believe it or not, people can smell God on us. They may not know that it's God they smell, but they know we carry something that others don't have. You see, it is impossible to hug God in prayer, in worship, in acts of service, and in deeds of kindness and not get His smell on you. People may only see our actions, but they are actually smelling the presence of God.

Like most couples, my wife and I have our preferred cologne and perfume. I always knew when she was close by because I could smell her presence and vice versa. One time I snuck up behind her to give her a scare, and she said, "I know you're here. I can smell you." I also knew when she was close to me. I loved the way she smelled. There were times when we hugged, and her perfume would cling to my shirt. During the day, I would catch the scent of her perfume, and it would remind me of the incredible union we shared with one another because of Christ being in our lives.

When I traveled overseas for extended periods of time, my wife would spray some of my cologne on her pillow. I would do the same with her perfume when she was away. This made us feel like our soulmate was lying next to us. I do it even more now since my sweet beloved and covenant partner has gone to be with Jesus. I can only imagine what heaven smells like. I am longing to know what she knows and experience what she is experiencing.

Here is what I am trying to get you to understand. It is impossible for us to hug God in worship and prayer without getting His smell on us. His smell is intoxicating. People can tell when we've been with Jesus. "Now when they saw the boldness of Peter and John, and perceived that they were uneducated and untrained men, they marveled. And *they realized that they had been with Jesus*" (Acts 4:13 NLT, emphasis added). People know. But they may not know what they know. It is impossible to hang around Jesus and not get His smell on you, any more than a chimney sweep can clean out a chimney and not get soot on themselves.

I stood beside my wife's bed with my hand placed lightly on her chest; she was about to take her last breath in this earthly realm. We were approaching our farewell moment. It was 4:17 a.m. No one was in the house but she and me and the Holy Spirit. It was quiet and so peaceful. We could literally feel the Lord's presence. I told my wife how much she was loved, what an incredibly loving and faithful wife she had been, how much our daughters and grandsons loved their Nanny Ann, what an incredible witness she had been to so many people, and allowing God to use her to make me into the kind of man I became today. Then she took her last breath here on earth and her first breath in heaven. The room was filled with the sweet aroma of God's presence. Not many couples get to have this kind of experience in their physical parting. Even though her departure was two years ago (as of this writing), it seems like it took place yesterday. I am still overcome with emotions every time I think about that special moment in April 2022. During these times, I can feel the Lord's arms around me as He hugs me with a firm but gentle embrace. Yes, I can smell His presence more now than I ever have. My beautiful wife Betty Ann hosted the Lord's presence like no one I have ever known. Those who really knew her will tell you the same thing.

Our Five Spiritual Senses

I spent the first twelve years of my life living in the country. I love country life. We moved to town when I was in the sixth grade, and I don't think I ever got over it. My parents took me, my brother, and two sisters out of the country to live on the other side of the city limits sign. This move was for my two sister's benefit, I might add. I think there is a song that says you can take the boy out of the country, but you cannot take the country out of the boy. I can vouch for the validity of that. My brother and I never did adjust to city life. We were country boys living in town, but the country was still living in us.

Even though I am now the same age as old people, I still remember the smells of country life. I love the smell of tomato fields. I can remember the times when we would be going home in the dark with all the car windows rolled down. At certain spots, we would pass large tomato fields. Even though we kids would be half asleep in the back seat of the car, we could tell how far we were from home by the smell of the tomato fields we passed because they were in close proximity to where we lived.

I also love the smell of fresh-cut grass and hay. There is something about that smell; it grabs my attention every time I get a whiff of it as does the smell of freshly popped popcorn, a smoking BBQ grill, spring rain showers, or a field of roses. The best sense of memory is smell, and this gift has been given to us by God.

In order for us to get a better understanding of our five spiritual senses, it would be wise to consult the Word of God for our information. The best place to begin is in the book of Hebrews. "For though by this time you ought to be teachers, you need someone to teach you again the first principles of the oracles of God; and you have come to need milk and not solid food. For everyone who partakes only of milk is *unskilled* in the word of righteousness, for he is a babe. But *solid food* belongs to those who are of full age, that is, those who *by reason of use* have *their senses* exercised *to discern* both good and evil" (Hebrews 5:12–14 NKJV, emphasis added). The writer of the book of Hebrews states unequivocally why there is so much immaturity within the family of faith when it comes to our spiritual senses and our giftings, no practice! This is what the word unskilled means, without trial. In other words, without practice. Have you noticed that we have no problem practicing medicine and law, but when it comes to practicing our faith, we have little to no interest? Not exercising our spiritual senses keeps us from enjoying many of our birthright privileges as children of God. It could be that we have not been taught, or we have no interest in knowing.

The following words are as appropriate today as they were when they were penned twenty-five to thirty years after Jesus's resurrection and ascension: "All of you should be teachers by now. You should be tutoring young believers in their walk with Christ." Teaching others about their faith walk with Christ was not a reality for these Hebrew believers. They were still in need of being taught the ABCs of the faith, the basic fundamental principles of living out their new creation lives, even though they had been believers for some time. It sounds familiar, doesn't it? There is a conspicuous absence of spiritual maturity in the body of Christ today. Practicing our faith is not high on our list of priorities. Because of this, a large percentage of believers have lost their effectiveness due to underuse and neglect of their spiritual senses. This can be reversed by exercising one's faith and getting better nutrition by feasting on the Word of God.

This would be a good time for us to take a glance at the unseen realm and see how it compares to the seen realm, and then we will come back to the Hebrews passage we started with. Hebrews 11:3 was one of many verses that stirred within me the desire to know who I am as a new creation in Christ. "By faith we understand that the worlds were framed by the word of God, so that *the things which are seen were not made of things which are visible*" (Hebrews 11:3 NKJV, emphasis added). Don't read this verse too fast. If you do, you might miss what the writer is saying. Things that we are able to see with our physical eyes were not made out of things that we can see. That's weird, isn't it? Keep tracking with me. If things we see are not made out of things that can be seen, it leaves us with one conclusion. The things we see are made out of things we can't see. This is not a play on words. It is what the Word of God says. If this is true, and I'm convinced it is, that means the unseen realm is more real than the seen realm. This stretches us out of our comfort zones. But it opens the door to understanding what Hebrews 5:14 is talking about, having our senses trained so we can discern what is good and what is evil. The writer who penned these words is not talking about natural senses; they are talking about our spiritual senses. Remember what Hebrews 11:3 tells us. The unseen realm is more real than the seen realm. It is also important for us not to confuse our spiritual senses with the spiritual gift of discernment mentioned in 1 Corinthians 12:10. This gift is for discerning spirits. Our spiritual senses have been given to us so we can know what is good and what is not good. All believers do not have the spiritual gift of discernment, but all of us children of God have been equipped with spiritual senses that enable us to discern what is right and what is not.

To discern is the spiritual characteristic of sound judgment for perceiving the difference between right and wrong, good and evil, truth and a lie, and identifying God's will and direction for our lives. I think the majority of the body of Christ suffers in these areas. Why? We haven't exercised our spiritual senses which has led to spiritual atrophy. Many within the body of Christ are not even aware they have spiritual senses. How can you practice something you don't know you have?

Each of our five physical senses is associated with a sense organ, each of which is responsible for sensing the environment and sending that information to the brain where it is interpreted as a sense. Illnesses like a cold or flu can impair our natural senses from doing what they are designed to do, especially our ability to smell and taste.

We use our five sensory perceptions every day whether we are cognizant of them or not. These abilities were intertwined in our human nature by our Creator at conception. We have been gifted with the ability to understand and interact with the environment using our natural senses. They are standard equipment.

What is true of our natural senses is even more true when it comes to our spiritual senses. When we had our born-from-above experience with Christ, we were given spiritual senses so we could understand, recognize, and interact with the spiritual realm. We are spiritual beings who live in bodies, not physical beings who have spirits. Because we are new creations in Christ, we can participate in things of the spirit.

Let's connect this with what we found hidden in Hebrews 11:3. Since the things we cannot see are more real than what we can see, this makes our spiritual senses more important than our natural ones. As new creations in Christ, we have the ability to connect with and relate to our spiritual environment. Think about that. Our Creator has made it possible for us to engage with the invisible realm by exercising our spiritual senses of sight, smell, taste, hearing, and touch. These spiritual senses are activated by faith, which is also a gift from God.

This may be confusing and a little befuddling to you if this is your first exposure to spiritual senses. But whatever you do, don't check out on me. Once this revelation begins to seep into your spirit, the presence of Christ in your life will be overpowering at times.

Here is the question that begs to be answered. Is it possible for us to touch God, smell God, hear God, taste God, and see God? The answer is a resounding yes. Let's take a quick trip through our spiritual sensory faculties and see what we have been gifted with and how we use our senses to connect with the spiritual realm; after all, we are spiritual beings.

The Spiritual Sense of Taste

Let's begin with the sense of taste. Listen to what David said about tasting the Lord. "Oh, *taste* and see that *the Lord* is good; Blessed is the man who trusts in Him" (Psalm 34:8 NLT, emphasis added)! Is it possible for us to taste the Lord? The man after God's own heart says we can, and he should know. And he tells us that the Lord tastes good.

The beautiful thing about the goodness of God is it's not seasonal. It's not a special dessert that is served on special occasions like Christmas, Easter, and other special days. His goodness is ever present. Keep the following in mind as you continue reading. Whatever God is, He is complete. Since He is good, He is completely good.

Tasting the Lord is to pull up to the table of the written Word and chow down. You don't need good table manners either—just roll up your sleeves and dig in. But you must eat for yourself. No one can benefit from you eating their food for them. They must eat for themselves to experience God's goodness. Tasting God is a personal matter. Once you have gorged yourself on His Word, digest it without compromise.

When we are not hungry, no food sounds good. This is why the Word of God says, "He [Jesus] has *filled the hungry with good things. And the rich [those not hungry] He has sent away empty*" (Luke 1:53 NLT, emphasis added). Those who eat the written Word of God voraciously and then meditate on what they read like a cow chewing its cud, will experience the presence of God like never before. Tasting God must be a personal experience. "For he satisfies the longing soul, and fills the hungry soul with goodness" (Psalm 107:9 NLT).

The Spiritual Sense of Hearing

The next stop on our quick trip through our spiritual sensory faculties is hearing. We apprehend the things in the spiritual realm by our sense of hearing. It is the presence of the Holy Spirit inhabiting our innermost being who alerts us to what is happening in the spiritual environment, just like our physical senses let us know what is happening in the world around us. Maybe we would benefit greatly by doing more listening than talking. Do you think God may have told us something profound when He created us with two ears and one mouth? It's a thought.

As a little boy, I heard my name called twice by an unfamiliar voice when I was probably eight or nine years old. I was all by myself when this happened. At that time, I had no clue what was going on. Both times it stopped me in my tracks. It was an audible voice. This happened over sixty-five years ago, but I can still hear that voice when I allow my thoughts to go back in time. The sound of that voice is locked in my spiritual memory system. Now I know who was calling my name. I was hearing the voice of God. I know this is way out there for some, but it's the unadulterated truth. With the advantage of many years and spiritual growth under my belt, I can look back on that moment and know with absolute certainty that it was God calling me into a relationship with him. It was His voice I heard.

It is the Holy Spirit dwelling inside our spirits that makes it possible for us to hear the things of the spirit. It would benefit all of us if we would be still and listen more attentively. There is no telling what we might hear God say to us.

The Spiritual Sense of Touch

Now that we have taken a quick glance at our spiritual senses of tasting and hearing, let's take a peep at touching. How in the world can that which has limits (that being us) touch something that is boundless? We touch God with our praise and prayers, with our good deeds, and with the exercising of our faith. God is not only approachable. He is touchable. "Then the Lord put forth his hand and touched my mouth, and the Lord said to me: Behold, I have put My words in your mouth" (Jeremiah 1:9 NLT). Since we are created in His image and are partakers of His divine nature (2 Peter 1:4), we can touch Him. Here is how we do it. "And the King will answer and say to them, 'Assuredly, I say to you, inasmuch as you did it to one of the least of these My brethren, you did it to me'" (Matthew 25:40 NLT). When we feed the hungry, clothe the naked, visit the sick, reach out to those who are in prison, and give drink to the thirsty, we are doing it to our Lord. When we touch others with hands of grace, we are touching God.

Some of the sweetest moments I have are when I sit still and bask in the Lord's presence. I have no agenda and no other motives except to sit quietly and feel His closeness. Once you have a close personal encounter with the Lord, you will be overawed. You will have nothing to say. These special moments are always available to us. It is up to us to redeem the time.

The Spiritual Sense of Sight

"I would have lost heart, unless I had believed that *I would see* the goodness of the Lord in the land of the living" (Psalm 27:13 NLT, emphasis added). Whether we are aware of it or not, we see the Lord every day of our lives. We can see Him in the small things as well as the large ones. He can be seen in the beautiful painted skies of an early morning sunrise and the glorious glow of an evening sunset. "The heavens declare the glory of God; and the firmament shows His handiwork" (Psalm 19:1 NLT).

Second Chronicles 7:14 (NLT) can be quoted by the vast majority of believers. It certainly gets my vote as being a great and timely verse. With our spiritual sense of sight in mind, I want us to read this verse again—slowly, "If My people who are called by My name will humble themselves, and pray and *seek My face*, and turn from their wicked ways, then I will hear from heaven, and will forgive their sin and heal their land." Our heavenly Father would not tell us to seek His face if it was impossible for us to see Him. We miss the opportunities after opportunities to see God's face because we are looking for a physical image and not a spiritual presence.

"Be still, and know that I am God" (Psalm 46:10 NLT). This verse tells us to do something that we find hard or don't want to do—be still. It's during these still moments that we begin to see the face of God all around us. He's been here all the time.

The Spiritual Sense of Smell

I saved the sense of smell for last because this is the subject of this chapter, the smell of God's presence. The fragrance of His closeness is easily detectable. If you ever get a whiff of Him, no one will have to tell you it's God you smell, and you certainly won't forget it. The aroma of His presence is unmistakable.

Let me give you my definition of what the word sense means in the spiritual realm. It is an ability to understand, recognize, value, or react to something, especially any of the five spiritual abilities to see, hear, smell, taste, and touch the unseen environment that the natural world does not have access to. When you had your born-again experience with Christ, you became a brand-new creation (2 Corinthians 5:17). This new creation is not natural; it is spiritual. Like our physical lives have natural senses, our spiritual lives have both. We can relate to the world around us through our physical senses, and we can connect with the spiritual unseen realm with our spiritual senses. Those who have not been born from above do not have this ability. They may consider those of us who have as being strange or even weird.

I would bet there have been times when you smelled God's breath and did not know what you were smelling. I know this is true if you have read the scriptures at all. Because we know that the written Word is the very breath of God, we can smell His breath as the Word we are reading is breathing on us (2 Timothy 3:16 TPT). When the Holy Spirit showed me this, it changed the way I read the Word. There are times I will stop reading and take a few slow deep breaths. When I do, I am keenly aware that He is not only with me, but He lives in me.

Once you recognize the smell of God, you will know that He is always with you. You will feel and smell His presence just like my wife and I could smell each other's presence by spraying each other's cologne and perfume on our pillows when we could not physically see one another. God will never leave or forsake us (Hebrews 13:5). Since He will always be with us, His smell will linger for eternity.

TWELVE

The Breath of God Is Our Constant Companion

Let your conduct be without covetousness; be content with such things as you have. For He himself said, 'I will never leave you nor forsake you.
—HEBREWS 13:5 (NLT)

I n 2007 I returned from a mission trip to Uganda, Africa. I and the team I was with had been away for over two weeks, and I was ready to get home. I wanted to see my beautiful wife and youngest daughter. Even though it was midnight when I got home, they both met me at the front door with big smiles on their faces and a warm embrace. My wife was cuddling an eight-week-old lab puppy in her arms. It was her JB gift to me. JB stands for *just because*. She and I were always surprising one another with JBs. We would sign the note or card with J.21—"I will not break my covenant with you" (Judges 2:1). Come Christmas time, we would tell each other that there was nothing we wanted or needed, and we meant it. We both had given and received gifts all year long just because we loved each other. We did not wait until birthdays, our anniversary, or Christmas. This was something we did our entire marriage.

His name was Duggan. That was the name given to the little JB puppy my wife blessed me with on my return from Africa. Duggan became my constant companion. For the first three years of his life, he was never out of my sight. He rode in my truck and slept next to my desk at the office. He had his own personal space in our home, and when we went on trips, guess who tagged along, Mr. Duggan. Wherever I went, Duggan was by my side. He knew my smell and the sound of my voice. When people would pet and talk to him, he would respond by wagging his tail rapidly and licking his chops. He loved attention, and he got a lot of it.

Duggan would not obey any command unless it came out of my mouth. He knew my voice and he would always respond immediately when I told him to do something. Some of my ornery friends tried to disprove Duggan's loyalty to me by giving him commands. They were not successful. He would not obey any voice other than his constant companion's—mine. He knew my voice, and he would listen to no other.

Duggan was an amazing dog. I can't tell you how many guys who hunted with me wanted to buy him. Some of them made generous offers. I had a couple of neighbors who told me they would love to have him for their own. A lot of people in our small town knew and loved Mr. Duggan. He was a once-in-a-lifetime pet and one phenomenal pheasant and quail dog. He was the best JB gift my beloved covenant partner ever gave me.

God's JB Gift to Us

God has given us a JB (just-because) gift, and He signed it with J.21: "I will never break My covenant with you" (Judges 2:1 NKJV). The gift He gave us has a name—Jesus. We didn't do anything to deserve or earn it either. "For *God so loved* the world that *He gave* His only begotten *Son*, that whoever believes in Him might be saved" (John 3:16 NKJV, emphasis added). What God has given us, the devil cannot take it away even though he will try. Whatever you do, don't let the devil try and convince you that God doesn't love you, or He only loves you conditionally. As long as you are obedient and loveable, all is well. But don't you ever stump your toe. If you do, your goose is cooked. When Satan whispers these words in your ear, breathe John 8:44 in his face. He knows what the breath of God smells like.

If you want to know the extent of God's love for you, all you have to do is look at the three crosses on Calvary's hill (Luke 23:33 NKJV). His gift to you is hanging on the middle one. What a JB gift! Once we accept and receive Jesus as our Lord and Savior, we don't need anything else. He is all we need. He is our constant companion. He is reliably present and always available. The Lord's love for us is invariable and unconditional. He is our life. Listen to the words of Jesus, "If you love Me, keep my commandments. And I will pray the Father, and He will give you another Helper, that *He may abide with you forever*—the Spirit of truth, whom the world cannot receive, because it neither sees Him nor knows Him; but you know Him, for *He dwells with you* and *will be in you. I will not leave you* orphans; I will come to you" (John 14:15–18 NKJV, emphasis added). These four verses sum up God's promise to us, He abides with us, He dwells in us, He will never leave us, and He signed this promise with His blood—J.21. Just think how special you are. God chose to be your constant companion. It doesn't get any better than that!

When we had our born-from-above experience with Jesus Christ, the breath of God moved in and took up permanent residence inside us. "The Spirit of God has made me, And the breath of the Almighty gives me life" (Job 33:3 NKJV). God breathed His life into us when we accepted His invitation to receive Him as our Lord and Savior. It is His breath that gives us life, and it is His breath that sustains our lives. The breath of God encapsulates both the spirit's power and divine purpose.

Our Constant Companion

The presence of God is not an atmosphere. It is a person. Glory is an atmosphere. We carry the glory, but we walk with His presence. This means that the breath of God is our constant companion. Knowing this as a living reality will give us the hope and strength that we need to navigate our way through anything that might challenge us in this life—anything.

The breath of God is our constant companion even if we feel like we are alone. The truth is as a child of God, we will never be alone. God has given His promise concerning that. "I will never leave you or forsake you" (Hebrews 13:5 NKJV). There may be times when we may not feel His presence, but that does not mean He is not with us. God cannot lie (Numbers 23:19, Titus 1:2, Hebrews 6:18).

Being alone is not the same thing as being lonely. Understanding what God said in Genesis 2:18 may help shed some light on this subject of being alone. "And the Lord God said, 'It is not good that man should be alone; I will make him a helper comparable to him'" (Genesis 2:18 NKJV). God did not say that it was not good for humans to be lonely. Yet this is exactly what most of us believe and teach. God said it was not good for humans to be alone.

Here is something we need to keep in mind when we read Genesis 2:18. Sin does not enter the picture until chapter 3. In chapter 2, Adam is living in a perfect environment with God so there is no way he could be lonely. This means that being alone may not mean what we have thought it did for all these years.

I was taught, as most people have, that when God saw that none of the animals was a suitable match for Adam, it was the reason He said that it was not good for a man to be lonely. But if it is, God made an oops if He created a man to be lonely. This sounds reasonable, but when you take a text out of its context, the only thing you will have left is a pretext. Let's look at the word *alone* in its context.

"God is love" (1 John 4:8 NKJV). You may be thinking, *Yes, He is but what does that have to do with Adam being lonely?* I'll give you the answer to that question in one word—everything. What does love do? Love gives. "For God *so loved* the world that He gave His only begotten Son, that whoever believes in Him should not perish but have everlasting life" (John 3:16 NKJV, emphasis added). Adam did not become a living soul, a speaking spirit until God breathed His life into him. This is a picture of love being given, and this love was expressed through the breath of God. If God doesn't breathe, there is no life. A body without life is just that, a body.

God is perfect within Himself. He doesn't need anyone to make Him complete. I will say this one more time because it is the key to understanding the difference between being lonely and alone: God is love, and what does love do—it gives. After God poured himself into Adam is when He said, "It is not good for man to be alone" (Genesis 2:18 NKJV). Adam needed someone he could pour himself into. Why? It's because love gives. The human race was not contaminated by sin until Genesis 3. Everything that took place before then happened in a perfect environment. Perfection has no room for loneliness.

Let me say this one more time. God did not say that it was not good for man to be lonely. He said it is not good that a man has all that he had been given and does not impart it to others. Let's say it together, "Love gives."

Silence Does Not Mean God Is Not Present

The presence of God cannot always be heard or felt. Sometimes these quiet moments are when God is speaking the loudest. How in the world can silence be the voice of God? Just because we can't feel His presence, it does not negate the truth that He is present. Be careful about believing the lie that says you have to *feel* the Lord's presence all the time. Sometimes we have to remind ourselves that He is the one who said He would never leave or forsake us. This is where faith kicks in. Can God be trusted?

I found myself in a season where I felt I needed to sit quietly before the Lord and listen to what He had to say. After all, prayer is a dialogue, not a monologue. When I pray, I have no problem talking, my shortcoming is giving Him time to respond. My plan was to sit on my back patio in the early morning hour while it was still dark so I could watch the new day wake up. Of course, I had a cup of coffee in my hands. I just wanted to listen to what God had to say.

The first morning, I did not hear God say a word or the second or third. I could not figure out why I was not having the divine encounter I had expected. On the fourth morning, things were different. As I sat quietly watching the light chase away the darkness, I began to see the trees reaching up toward heaven as if they were clapping their hands, the sky declared the Creator's handiwork, I could hear the birds worshipping involuntarily, and then all of a sudden, I was aware that I was hearing God speak. His voice wasn't what I had envisioned it to be. He was speaking to me through His creation. All of a sudden, I was overwhelmed with His presence. He was there all the time. I did not have my spiritual ears tuned in to the right frequency. "Be still, and know that I am God" (Psalm 46:10 NKJV). Some of the best moments we can have with God are when we are quiet and still.

I still meet with Him every morning on my back patio. I sit quietly with my eyes and ears open as He speaks to me about what the new day has to offer. His voice has gotten clearer and stronger. This time has become very special to me, and I do everything in my power to keep distractions from interfering with it. Silence does not mean God is not present. All we have to do is sit still, close our mouths, and open our eyes.

God's Promise to Us

"God is striding ahead of you. He's right there with you. He won't let you down; he won't leave you. Don't be intimidated. Don't worry" (Deuteronomy 31:8 MSG). This verse covers all the bases. God will go before us, He's with us, He won't let us down, and He will never leave us. It's no wonder we are told not to worry. The breath of God is with us no matter what is going on in our lives. When the sun is shining, He is there. When it's dark and gloomy, He is with us. There is absolutely nothing that can contend with our God. He has no rivals. This is so comforting to know.

David, a man after God's own heart, wrote these words: "Yea, though I walk through the valley of the shadow of death, I will fear no evil; For You are with me; Your rod and Your staff, they comfort me" (Psalm 23:4 NKJV). Where is God when we are going through valleys that have the smell of death in them? David tells us He is with us. The Lord doesn't walk with us during the good times and then bail on us when things get tough. His shepherd's crook makes us feel secure. What keeps us going through our valley walks is knowing our heavenly Father will never abandon us.

During my lifetime, I have had some death-valley experiences. Even as I write this book, I am going through an emotional season. My precious covenant partner folded her earthly tent for the last time twenty-one months ago as of this writing. She is absent from her earthly body, but she's present with her Lord. Every day has its challenges. Jesus did not lie to us when He said that as long as we are in this world, we will have troubles. It's not if we have downturns, it's when. No matter what path you are on, no one can walk it for you, and only one can walk it with you: the one who said He would never leave or forsake you. It is His breath that keeps us on our feet. It is His breath that lifts our spirits. It is His breath that gives us hope, and it is His breath that gives us purpose.

Everything Obeys the Breath of God

In Matthew 8, Jesus gives a short teaching on the cost of discipleship. It was not well received by His audience. After He finished His lesson, He got on a boat, and His disciples joined Him. "And suddenly a great tempest arose on the sea so that the boat was covered with the waves. But He was asleep. Then His disciples came to Him and awoke Him, saying, "'Lord, save us! We are perishing!' But He said to them, 'Why are you fearful, O you of little faith?' Then He arose and rebuked the winds and the sea, and there was a great calm. So the men marveled, saying, 'Who can this be, that even the winds and the sea obey Him'" (Matthew 8:24–27 NKJV).

Try to picture this scene in your mind. Where was Jesus when the disciples found themselves in this bad storm? He was in the boat asleep. How was it possible for Jesus to sleep in the middle of a storm on the sea of Galilee? A storm was raging and the lives of those in the boat with Him were in jeopardy. They were full of fear, but Jesus was totally at peace. He was able to sleep in what created fear in others.

Jesus rebuked the wind and the water with His breath. It amazes me how quickly the elements obeyed the voice of their Creator. I wonder what kind of life we would experience if we were this quick to obey when God spoke to us. This is something to ponder on. The breath of His mouth quieted the winds and calmed the water. The elements had no problem recognizing Jesus's voice. After all, it was His breath that gave life to everything. All of creation came into existence by God's spoken Word, and it is His voice that creation responds to. The disciples were awestruck. They were amazed at how the howling winds and the raging sea obeyed without hesitation.

"But [Jesus] said to them, 'Why are you fearful, O you of little faith?'" (Matthew 8:26 NKJV). I think I know the answer to Jesus's question. The disciples felt they had met their waterloo, and to add to their anxiety, they felt Jesus really didn't care. Their logic made sense because Jesus was sound asleep while they were in full panic mode.

It is impossible to go through life and not experience storms of varying sizes. There are moments when things may look like they are totally out of control, and we are not sure we will see tomorrow. In the midst of our difficulties and perplexing situations, we may feel the Lord is not in the boat with us. We can't hear His voice or feel His presence. Feelings of hopelessness rage through our souls like a runaway freight train. It is during times and seasons like these that we must remind ourselves of what the writer of Hebrews said, "This hope we have as an anchor of the soul, both sure and steadfast and which enters the Presence behind the veil" (Hebrews 6:19 NKJV). I am well aware that I've talked about this verse in chapters 8 and 10, but the truth of it can't be emphasized enough. It may be the best takeaway from this book. When Jesus is the anchor of your life, you are secure no matter how severe your situations and circumstances may be.

Jesus is our anchor regardless of how we may be feeling during our storms. An anchor does not keep storms from ranging, but it will keep the vessel steady in the midst of the storm. It's not about feeling His presence that keeps us from waving the white flag of surrender, but it is knowing He is always present with us because He has taken up permanent residence in our lives. As our anchor, He will keep us grounded and connected to what matters most, no matter how confused and challenging life gets. His breath will always be our constant companion.

A True Companion

"Friends come and friends go, but a true friend sticks by you like family" (Proverbs 18:24 MSG). If you are blessed to have a true friend in your life, count yourself blessed. A legitimate friend is a rare commodity. A friend is someone who knows everything about you but still loves you and will be loyal in season and out of season when life is good and when life seems to be falling apart. A legitimate friend is hard to find.

You are blessed and may not even know it. No person could have a better friend than Jesus. He knows more about you than you do yourself, and He's still madly in love with you. He knows your deepest, darkest secrets, and He doesn't talk about you behind your back. He wants nothing but the best for you. He will always speak truth to you in love. You will never have to wonder if He's in your corner or not. Jesus is a true companion.

The value of a true friend is revealed during tumultuous times. I'm sure we all have had fair-weather friends—people who are with us when everything is good. But when storm clouds begin to gather, they can't be found even with the help of the FBI or the CIA, not Jesus. He is with us through thick and thin. We never have to wonder if He is with us.

A genuine friend will speak the truth to you in love. The only thing Jesus can speak is truth because He is truth. Truth will never change; therefore, His friendship and companionship with you will never change. Jesus speaks truth to build us up not tear us down.

Jesus loves you with unconditional love, no strings attached. When you know how much He loves you, you can't help but love Him back. Love never fails (1 Corinthians 13:4–8). He understands your feelings without asking, and He will always help you without ulterior motives. You'll never have a friend who loves you like He does.

Most importantly, a friend will be willing to lay down their lives for you. "But God demonstrated His own love toward us, in that while we were still sinners, Christ died for us" (Romans 5:8 NKJV). This verse is stunning. When we did not want anything to do with Jesus, God put His love on display for us by sending Jesus to the cross, taking our place and dying our death. What a friend we have in Jesus.

"What a Friend We Have in Jesus" was written by Joseph M. Scriven as a poem in 1855. This is the first verse:

> What a Friend we have in Jesus
> All our sins and griefs to bear!
> What a privilege to carry everything
> to God in prayer!

We will never have a better friend than Jesus. He will never abandon us no matter what happens to us in this lifetime. He is our friend and constant companion.

THIRTEEN

The Healing Breath of Jesus

Bless the Lord, O my soul; And forget not all His benefits: Who forgives all your iniquities, Who heals all your diseases.
—PSALM 103:2–3 (NKJV)

One of the most misunderstood subjects in the Bible, and I might add, confusing, is healing. Why is it that some people appear to be healed, and others are not? I think most of us have witnessed both in our walk with the Lord. By no means am I presenting myself as a know-it-all when it comes to physical healing. I would be very cautious about listening to someone who says they have it all figured out. What I will share with you in this chapter on the healing breath of Jesus is what I believe the spirit of God has shown me in this season of my life. Not long ago my beautiful covenant partner was escorted to her heavenly home. She had battled cancer for almost seven years and fought tenaciously. She was a woman with undaunted faith. Over the years I saw her lay hands on an untold number of women who were facing all kinds of physical challenges. Many of these ladies had a manifestation of their healing. Some did not.

After my wife departed this earthly realm, I began to search the scriptures to better understand physical healing. I have a burning passion to know why some people have a manifestation of healing and others don't even though they may be strong in their faith. I asked the Holy Spirit to help me see what I haven't seen and to know what I don't know. What I'm going to share with you in this chapter is what I am convinced the spirit of God has revealed to me about this subject—so far. I am convinced this journey will continue until I make my transition from this earthly realm to the heavenly realm. Then I will know as I am known.

As you continue reading, keep this in mind, the unseen realm (spiritual) is more real than the seen realm (natural). Let me say it this way, what we can't see is more real than what we can see (Hebrews 11:3). Our faith in the scriptures is the lens that gives us the ability to see the unseeable.

There are two scriptures that most of the family of faith are familiar with. The first one is Isaiah 53:5. The last part of this verse says (NKJV, emphasis added), "And by His stripes *we are healed.*" The second scripture is 1 Peter 2:24 (NKJV, emphasis added), "By whose stripes *you were healed.*" We are healed, and we were healed. This sounds to me like we are healed, and we were healed. Duh. To me, any other position is untenable.

Everything you read from this point on is an attempt to plumb the depths of these two scriptures about healing. It may be diametrically opposed to what you have understood physical healing to be. Once again, I want to go on record that I do not have this healing thing figured out. Someday we all will know, but until then, let's keep digging.

Guilt Caused by False Accusations

With many years of ministry under my belt, I have ministered to untold numbers of individuals who were living under heavy oppression caused by guilt. They had prayed for the healing of a friend or loved one, and there was no manifestation of their healing. Instead of being healed, some died. They were told that if they had more faith, the people they prayed for would have been healed and still be alive. This is a false accusation. This lie is whispered in our ears by the enemy. The only fruit comments like this can produce is false guilt. The chances are good that the people who have been told this no longer pray for people to be healed. After all, they don't have enough faith.

God's Measure of Faith

This would be a good time to address the faith issue. What do you have that was not given to you by God? I will provide you with the answer to this question—not one thing. If this is true and there is biblical proof to support it, then the faith we have is actually not ours. According to Galatians 2:20, we live by the faith of another. If we have a shortage of faith, then it's God's fault that the people we prayed for were not healed. He didn't give us as much faith as He gave others. This needs to be debunked.

"For I say, through the grace given to me, to everyone who is among you, not to think of himself more highly than he ought to think, but to think soberly, as *God has dealt to each one a measure of faith*" (Romans 12:3 NKJV, emphasis added). God has given each one of us a measure of faith. But maybe the measure He gave me is not as big as the measure He gave you.

Let's take a look at what the measure of God is. In Psalm 23:5, David says that his cup runs over. He did not say that God fills his cup to the brim. His cup overflows. There's God's measure. In Luke 15, a father received his prodigal son with open arms who came to his senses and returned home where he belonged. He gave his servants instructions to kill the fated calf and prepare it for his son's homecoming celebration. Did you notice that it wasn't just a calf?

It was a fated calf. There's God's measure. The robe that was draped over the shoulders of this young man was not just a robe, but it was the best robe. There's God's measure. Listen to the words of Paul in his letter to the Ephesians. "Now to Him who is able to do *exceedingly abundantly above all* that we ask or think, according to the power that works in us" (Ephesians 3:20 NKJV, emphasis added). It is not in God's nature to give less to some of his children than He has given the rest. The point I'm trying to get across is that we have been gifted with all the faith we need. God did not shortchange any of us. His faith has been given to us as kingdom currency. He is not going to give you more faith than He gave me. God's only measure of giving is more than enough. We don't have a faith issue. Our issue is not knowing what God has so graciously given us.

When you accepted and received Jesus as your Lord and Savior, God breathed His life into you. The life of God lives on the inside of you in the person of the Holy Spirit. To get an understanding of what this looks like, picture God breathing His breath into the nostrils of the first Adam in Genesis 2:7. Then and only then was when the first man became a living soul. It was God's breath that gave him life. This is exactly what the last Adam (Jesus) did to you when you had your born-from-above experience. God breathed His life into you and took up permanent residence. Let me say it another way—God is not a part of our lives; He is our lives (Colossians 3:4). As we let this truth sink in, let's keep praying that God does not stop breathing. You see, the very breath we have in our lungs is a gift from God. Do you remember the question I asked earlier and then gave you the answer? What do you have that was not given to you by God? And the answer is if you said not one thing, move to the head of the class.

God doesn't give us His life on an installment plan, a little here and a little there. When He took up residence in you, it was for all time. You now have eternal life living on the inside of you. Included with this life is God's measure of faith. You can't see it (manifestation), but it's there.

Sight Is Not a Prerequisite for Faith

"Now faith is the substance of things hoped for, the evidence of things not seen" (Hebrews 11:1 NKJV). Faith is believing what we can't see with our physical eyes. If this is true, then sight is not a requirement for validating our faith. A manifestation of healing is sight. If we see a manifestation of healing after we pray for someone, we are quick to say a person was healed. But when there is no manifestation of healing, we believe a person was not healed. What happened to we are healed and we were healed? Is the truth of these two scriptures of healing based on sight, what we can see and what we can't? It is if the criteria for believing a person is healed is based on a manifestation. Maybe we need to be thanking God for our healing and not begging Him to heal us. Whether or not there is a manifestation, we are healed. How do we know? God's Word tells us we are healed, and we were healed, no matter what we see or don't see with our physical eyes.

Unknowingly we fall into the trap that says we must have sight to support our faith. This actually subverts faith. Faith is the evidence of things not seen. So what do we do when we pray for someone's healing, and there is no manifestation they are healed? We have added conditions to faith. I'll only believe a person is healed when I see it. If I don't see it, they are not healed. I'm going to keep repeating what Isaiah 53:5 and 1 Peter 2:24 say, we are healed and we were healed. The manifestation of healing is not mentioned in either scripture. Could it be that sight is not a part of the healing equation?

Gifts of Healing

In Paul's first letter to the Corinthian church, he addresses the subject of spiritual gifts—empowerment. Not everyone in the body of Christ has been gifted with the same gifts.

God's gifts are handed out everywhere; but they all originate in God's Spirit. God's various ministries are carried out everywhere; but they all originate in God's Spirit. God's various expressions of power are in action everywhere; But God himself is behind it all. Each person is given something to do that shows who God is: Everyone gets in on it, everyone benefits. All kinds of things are handed out by the Spirit, and to all kinds of people! The variety is wonderful:

> wise counsel
> clear understanding
> simple trust
> healing the sick
> miraculous acts
> proclamation
> distinguishing between spirits
> tongues
> interpretation of tongues.

All these gifts have a common origin, but are handed out one by one by the One Spirit of God. He decides who gets what, and when. (1 Corinthians 12:1–11 MSG, emphasis added)

Have you noticed that all through this passage, we are reminded again and again that God is the giver of all spiritual endowments? He decides who gets what gift. Among those mentioned in this passage are the gifts of healing (1 Corinthians 12:9 NKJV). Many people have asked this question, "If I have been empowered with a particular spiritual gift, is it possible for other gifts to flow through me?" The answer is *absolutely*. Again who is the giver of these gifts? God can do whatever He wants to do and when He wants to do it.

If there is a need for the expression of a particular gift, He can and will use anyone as a conduit for the expression of that gift.

This would be a good time to slay a giant of misunderstanding about healing. If a believer does not have the gift(s) of healing(s), can they pray for someone's healing and there be a manifestation? The answer is an unequivocal yes. Here are the words of Jesus: "[Believers] they shall take up serpents; and if they drink anything deadly, it will by no means hurt them; *they shall lay hands on the sick, and they shall recover*" (Mark 16:18 NKJV, emphasis added). I am well aware that many theologians (I'm not even close to being one) say that some of the earliest manuscripts (Codex Sinaiticus and Codex Vaticanus) do not include Mark 16:9–20. If they are correct, then verse 18 is null and void. We can't lay hands on the sick and infirm and see them healed. This chapter on the healing breath of God is not an apologetic on the canonicity of the scriptures. I refuse to allow myself to be entrapped by qualifying what is the Word of God and what is not. I'll leave that task to others. As for me and my house, we're going with the word we have, and our word says that as believers, we can lay our hands on the sick, and they shall recover. That's the end of the conversation.

The Breath of God Is Our Healing

When you accepted the Lord's invitation to life, He breathed His life into you. You got all of Him at that moment, and that includes healing. God is not only our healer; He is our healing. God's life is in you, and there is no sickness in Him. You were healed you are healed. I know this sounds like spiritual sci-fi. The reason it does is because it takes us into the realm of the spiritual, and that makes us uncomfortable. We are so consumed by our physical surroundings that having a conversation about what we can't see makes us nervous and suspicious. This is an indication that sight is more important to us than we want to admit. If we can't see it, then how do we really know it exists? Anyone who has the audacity to embrace the spiritual over the natural is considered weird and untrustworthy. People like this are dreamers. They do not live in reality. We need to stay away from these folks. They may lead us astray. This is why people are quick to say that we should not be so heavenly minded that we are of no earthly good. The truth is, we are not impacting our world like we should and could because we are not heavenly minded enough.

Does the Word of God become suspect when it talks about believing in what we can't see? "For we walk by faith, not by sight" (2 Corinthians 5:7 NKJV). The Message rendition of this verse says, "It's what we trust in but don't yet see that keeps us going" (2 Corinthians 5:8 MSG). If we have cautious mistrust in people who make the claim that the unseen is more real than the seen, how are we going to handle what God says about it? His word declares that sight is not what causes us to believe, but it is faith in what we can't see because God said it. What we don't see is what keeps us going. I'm not giving you a man's opinion on this subject. God's Word makes this claim.

Let me connect what I just said to the theme of this chapter. If you pray for healing and there is no manifestation (sight) of it, is that person healed? I think in most circles, you would get a no answer. I realize this is logical reasoning. If it can't be seen, it must not have happened. But we must acknowledge that what God says is the final word on anything, not our reasoning. God's Word on healing says that we are healed and were healed (Isaiah 53:5, 1 Peter 2:4). The reason this makes no sense to the majority of us is that we are more comfortable with looking at things from an earthly perspective than we are from a spiritual point of view. I think this would be a good time to insert a word of reminder. This has been said a couple of times already. We are spiritual beings who have souls, and we live in a body. We are not physical beings who have spirits. It may be time for us to start living and thinking about who we really are.

Let me stretch you a little more. Did you know that we are in two places at the same time: here on this earth and seated with

Christ in heaven (Ephesians 2:6)? This means we can think two ways, worldly or heavenly. There is heaven's perspective, and there's this physical world's perspective. It is possible to view things from our position in Christ who is seated at the right hand of the Father, or we can look at things from our earthly habitation. We have the worldly part figured out pretty well, but we need a little more practice on our heavenly thinking.

Jesus talks about death the same way He talks about healing. "Whosoever believes in me shall never die" (John 11:26 NKJV). We see people die every day, and for many of these, we have personally prayed for their healing. And Jesus tells us that if we believe in Him, we will never die. Yes, He did. There is no difference between what Jesus said about death and what He said about healing. We will never die. We are healed, and we were healed. We don't need physical sight to confirm the Word of God. Maybe, just maybe, we can trust His word on both issues. Since we will never die, sickness and disease have no power to take our lives.

Why Do We Battle Physical Diseases If We Are Healed?

We live in a contaminated world where it rains on the just and the unjust. "[But I say to you] that you may be sons of your Father in heaven; for He makes His sun rise on the evil and on the good, and sends rain on the just and on the unjust" (Matthew 5:45 NKJV). Good things and bad things happen to Christians and nonbelievers alike. It's because the seed of the first man was corrupted by his disobedience, and this corrupted seed was passed on to the entire human race.

Even though we're in the world we are not of the world. Listen closely to what Jesus said to Pilate and not just what He said, but what He did not say. "Jesus answered, 'My kingdom is not of this world. If My kingdom were of this world, My servants would fight, so that I should not be delivered to the Jews; but now My kingdom is not from here" (John 19:36 NKJV). Jesus did not say that His kingdom was not in this world. He said His kingdom was not of this world. This is true of us who are a part of His kingdom. We are aliens in this earthly realm. You may have never thought of yourself as being an alien. You are if you are a child of God. Our citizenship is in heaven. Some day we are going home. Until then, let's start thinking like citizens of heaven.

When I pray for myself or someone who is battling health issues, I do ask for a manifestation of the healing they already have, and many times it happens. Other times, it doesn't. But I believe they are healed even when there is no physical sight to support what I believe. This destroys all thoughts about not having enough faith when there is not a visible expression of their healing.

Open Our Eyes Lord That We May See

Out of anger at having his secret plans for destroying Israel exposed by the prophet Elisha, the king of Syria sent a great army to surround the city of Dothan where the prophet lived—a whole army after one man. Elisha's servant arose early in the morning and went outside. This was when he saw (physical sight) this great army that had gathered. This young man told Elisha what he saw and asked him what they were going to do. Listen to Elisha's weird answer, "Do not fear, for those who are with us are more than those who are with them" (2 Kings 6:16 NKJV). The focus of the servant was on the seen realm. The man of God had his spiritual eyes set on the unseen realm. What we can't see is more real than what we can see.

Is it possible for us to shift our focus from the natural to the spiritual? Well, let's see. "And Elisha prayed, and said, 'Lord, I pray, open his eyes that he may see.' Then the Lord opened the eyes of the young man, and he saw. And behold, the mountain was full of horses and chariots of fire all around Elisha" (2 Kings 6:17 NKJV). The prayer Elisha prayed for his servant is nothing short of amazing,

"Open his eyes that he may see." We know he could see because he saw the mighty army that had them surrounded. His sight is what planted the seed of fear in his heart. It is obvious it was this young man's spiritual vision that allowed him to see the great heavenly host that had the king of Syria's army surrounded.

Can this be applicable to physical healing? I am convinced it can be. Oftentimes we are able to see the manifestation of healing that we prayed for, and at other times, we can't. This is when we need to have our spiritual sight activated, and this is done by the Word of God. And the word says we were and we are healed even when we can't see it.

We Are Healed from All Our Diseases

If we could interview someone who is now in the presence of God about healing, what do you think they might say? When they were still in this world their physical healing did not manifest even though they were prayed for by people who were strong in faith. Would it sound something like this, "I know you didn't see my healing with your eyes, but let me tell you I am healed and I was healed." Some day you will see.

I think it would be appropriate to end this chapter with the scripture I began it with. "Bless the Lord, O my soul, And forget not all His benefits; Who forgives all your iniquities, *Who heals all your diseases*" (Psalm 103:2–3 NKJV, emphasis added). What incredible benefits we have as the children of God, which includes healing for all our diseases.

God Is the Life inside of Life

The Spirit can make life. Sheer muscle and willpower
don't make anything happen. Every word I have spoken
to you is a Spirit–word, and so it is life-making.
—JOHN 6:63 (MSG)

I realize the title of this chapter may seem a little strange at first read. But once you see the core of what it says, you will realize that without God there is no life. God is the life inside of life. "Everything comes from him; Everything happens through him; Everything ends up in him. Always glory! Always praise! Yes. Yes. Yes" (Romans 11:36 MSG). This sounds to me like maybe God is the life of everything that exists in this world and beyond. Since the Word of God says He is, He gets my vote.

Being able to breathe is not something we give much attention to until our ability to breathe is impaired. Gasping and not being able to take a breath can put you in a state of panic. Sometimes a person may even lose consciousness if the blow to their diaphragm is hard enough. This is often called getting the air knocked out of them. Life is filled with these events.

From my junior high days through high school, basketball was my life. I lived to play this sport. I had an addiction to the smell and noise of a gymnasium. The pounding of a leather ball on a hardwood floor was music to my ears. Basketball practice was as enjoyable for me as playing a game. I loved the sport.

One day in practice, a lot of taunting was being bantered about by most of the members of the team. Things got a little heated, to say the least. Tempers escalated to the point where punches were exchanged. I got blindsided by a punch to the diaphragm that took the breath out of my lungs. I immediately hit the floor, holding my stomach and gasping for air. Even though this happened over sixty years ago, I remember it as if it happened last week. You don't forget something as painful as that was. I came very close to passing out. The pain and panic I felt were so intense I didn't think I would ever recover, but I did.

Sudden Loss of Air

Sometimes life experiences can be so traumatic that we feel like our spiritual breath has been knocked out of us. The pain caused by these events may leave us wondering if we ever recover, will we ever breathe again? Since God is the life inside of life, we can be assured that we will survive any and all challenges that come our way because He will never cease to exist. God is eternal, meaning He had no beginning and He has no end. He has always been, and He will always be. He said this about Himself on several occasions—"I Am," not I was or I will be. He said, "I Am."

Life can be so unpredictable. Some days we are soaring in the clouds, and some days we are swimming among the seaweeds. Everything can be going great, and then all of a sudden *bam*, our spiritual diaphragm takes a blow leaving us wheezing. One day we look like a contender, and the next day we feel like a pretender. Life is filled with seasons, and the seasons are always changing. This does not mean you are doing something wrong. It's part and parcel of this thing called life.

The apostle Paul knew something about the unfairness of life.

He shared this in his second letter to the church in Corinth. He begins with the words,

> I know I sound like a madman, but I have served him [Christ] far more! I have worked harder, been put in prison more often, been whipped times without number, and faced death again and again. Five different times the Jewish leaders gave me thirty-nine lashes. Three times I was beaten with rods. Once I was stoned. Three times I was shipwrecked. Once I spent a whole night and day adrift at sea. I have traveled on many long journeys. I have faced dangers from rivers and robbers. I have faced danger from my own people, the Jews, as well as from the Gentiles. I have faced dangers in the cities, in deserts, and on the seas. And I have faced danger from men who claim to be believers but are not. I have worked long and hard, enduring many sleepless nights. I have been hungry and thirsty and have often gone without food. I have shivered in the cold, without enough clothing to keep me warm. Then, besides all this, I have the daily burden of my concern for all the churches. (2 Corinthians 11:23–28 NLT, emphasis added)

Let me sum up what Paul is saying to the believers who lived in Corinth. Living a life that is pleasing to the Lord is a piece of cake. There's nothing to it. Life is filled with only good things if you have surrendered your life to the Lord. A child of God will never have to struggle while living in the earthly realm. Life is fair, so throw all caution to the wind and live it up.

I bet most of you, if not all, are thinking, *This dude is off his meds*. That is not what Paul said. It's totally opposite. You are right if that's what you thought when you read my summation of what

Paul said to his fellow Christians. Believe it or not, I'm really not off my medications. I'm trying to get your attention to make a point. Life can be tough and unfair at times. It is possible to be totally committed to your walk with the Lord and have unfavorable things happen to you. It's not uncommon to feel trapped and oppressed by what is going on in our lives. When this happens, we need to remind ourselves that God is the life inside of life. He is not only the one who gives me life, but He is my life. "For in him *we live* and *move* and *exist*" (Acts 17:28 NLT, emphasis added).

I heard years ago that tough times don't last tough people do (Robert H. Schuller). This statement is about spiritual toughness—not physical strength. The longer I live and the more seasons of life I experience, the truth of what Schuller said makes more sense. The physically weak can be spiritually strong. And the physically strong can be spiritually weak.

As I told you in the last chapter, I have a burning desire to understand why there is a manifestation of healing for some people we pray for, and others don't. I know a lot more about healing now than I did before, but I still have a lot more to learn. One of the things I've discovered is that Jesus is not only our healer He is our healing. The written Word declares Him to be a great physician. He is the only one who can heal, but He is more than a healer. There is no difference between these two declarations. Jesus is my healing, and He is the life inside my life.

How to Survive Suffocating Moments

When I received the phone call from the school system where my firstborn daughter was a speech pathologist to let me know she was taken by ambulance to the hospital, it felt like I was being suffocated. All the emotional air that was inside of me felt like it was being squeezed out. What the school officials could not tell me over the phone was that my twenty-five-year-old daughter had died. When I walked through the emergency doors of the hospital and saw all the people crying, shaking their heads in unbelief, praying, and consoling one another, I knew the report was not good. A hospital staff member ushered me back to the room where my daughter was. I will never forget that suffocating moment when I walked into that room and saw my beautiful girl lying motionless on the table. The attending physicians and medical staff did everything within their power to save her life but were helpless. To add more pain to this testimony, my daughter Melanie was only two weeks away from giving birth to my first grandson. Because of oxygen deprivation, he only lived for twenty minutes.

To keep from losing complete control of my mental faculties, I began to quote the scriptures out loud to myself. Unknowingly I was breathing in and out spiritual air. At that time, there was no Passion Translation of 2 Timothy 3:16, "God has transmitted his very substance into every Scripture, for it is God-breathed." I was actually breathing in God's life. It is His life that gives life, and it is His life that sustains life. The only reason we exist is because of His life living on the inside of us.

King David knew something about suffocating moments. In the book of Psalms, he pens these words, "Even when the way goes *through* Death Valley, I'm not afraid when you walk at my side. Your trusty shepherd's crook makes me feel secure" (Psalm 23:4 TPT, emphasis added). God may not deliver us from death-valley experiences, but He has promised to take us through every one of them. There is one thing we can always count on when life throws us a curve. God will walk with us through every low point we may encounter. He will never run out on us. He is a good shepherd, and He is madly in love with His sheep.

One of the first verses I internalized when I got serious about my walk with Christ was Psalm 119:11 (NLT, emphasis added), "I have *hidden* your word in my *heart*, that I might not sin against you." This verse does not say we are to memorize the scriptures or just quote it. It needs to become a part of our character. It's not about how much scripture you know. It's about how much scripture you live.

When the Word of God is only in our heads, we have it. But when the Word is hidden in our hearts, it has us. We must never forget that God transmitted His very substance and His essence into every scripture. Breathing in and out the written Word of God is inhaling and exhaling the life of God. He is our life (Colossians 3:4).

There are times when the valleys we find ourselves walking through are so painful that we are not sure we will survive. Feelings of isolation consume us. We feel all alone and hopeless. The enemy of our souls will try to convince us that these feelings are true, that we are totally isolated. The voice whispering in our ears tells us not to expect a good outcome. Never forget what Jesus said about the devil; he is a liar and the father of all lies. This is why we need to breathe in the Word of God. "I will never leave you nor forsake you" (Hebrews 13:5 NKJV). God's promise to us is that we will never be alone even when we feel like we are. He is with us during the good times, bad times, and all the times in between. God is the life inside of life.

Out of the Abundance of the Heart, the Mouth Speaks

After Jesus healed a demon-possessed, blind, and mute man, who had been brought to him, the Pharisees accused Jesus of receiving His power to do this from Beelzebub, the ruler of demons. Jesus gives them a pretty stern lesson on identity. Then He says to these self-righteous synagogue-choir boys, "For out of the abundance of the heart the mouth speaks" (Matthew 12:34 NKJV). Jesus tells us that speech is actually a heart issue. Our mouths will expose what's in our hearts. Like a fruit defines a tree, our speech defines us. The heart has a voice. Again I remind all of us how important it is to hide the Word of God in our hearts, not our heads. When the pressures of life begin to squeeze us, whatever comes out is what's on the inside. "Thy word have I hid in my heart" (Psalm 119:11 NKJV). If we are hiding God's Word in our hearts, we will breathe out His word, which is His breath—which is His life.

It is impossible for a person to hide their true character for any length of time. If you really want to know someone, don't focus on their outside appearance. Listen to what is on the inside of them. Their true nature is revealed by what they say. All of us, there are no exceptions, will be exposed to the content of our hearts expressed through their mouths. "Guard your heart above all else, for it determines the course of your life" (Proverbs 4:23 NLT).

"For by your words you will be justified, and by your words you will be condemned" (Matthew 12:37 NKJV). Here's my personal rendition of Matthew 12:37. What we say will validate or invalidate us. I love how the New Living Translation translates this verse. "The words you say will either acquit you or condemn you." Ouch! Here's the bottom line. Speech can be our greatest ally or our worst enemy. We make the call.

Here's a little exercise you can do that will let you know what a person really believes. During a conversation with someone, listen to how they connect words, clauses, and sentences. Start eavesdropping on the conjunctions a person uses when you're talking to them. Become a conjunction secret agent. You can do this without them ever knowing they are under surveillance by a grammar cop.

The main coordinating conjunctions are and, or, and but with *but* being the main conjunction that reveals what a person truly believes. Whatever a person says, listen to how they end their statement because it will tell you what they really believe. Here's an example. "I know the word of God declares that I am healed and I believe it, but I've been fighting this physical issue for several years now and I'm not sure I'll ever get over it." Even though this individual says they believe they are healed, they are not convinced they are. You know this by what they say after the conjunction but. Jesus might have been on to something when He said, "For whatever is in your heart determines what you say" (Matthew 12:34 NLT). The hidden things in our hearts are revealed every time we open our mouths and speak. The mouth is the pump that pulls the unseen contents of our hearts out into the open. We don't have to worry about people putting words into our mouths; our hearts will take care of that.

Then God Said

When you read the history (His story) of creation found at the beginning of the first book of the Bible, there are three words that cannot be ignored, "Then God said." Nothing existed until God spoke it into being. Not one thing. God literally breathed the terrestrial realm into existence. This makes Him the life in all life because without Him, there would be no life. Since this is true, everything God spoke into existence by His word is also sustained by His word. Let this sink in. Everything is held together by the breath of God. This includes every person on this planet. I've quoted Colossians 3:4 a couple of times already in previous chapters, but it needs to be repeated one more time because it is the foundation this chapter is built. "When Christ, *who is our life* appears, then you also will appear with Him in glory" (emphasis added). Since He is our life, we have no life without Him.

"By faith, we see *the world called* [breathed] *into existence by God's word* [breath], what we see created by what we don't see" (Hebrews 11:3 MSG, emphasis added). Eight times in the thirty-one verses of Genesis 1 these three words appear, "Then God said." The number eight is the number for completion and the beginning of a new order. In the creation account, the eighth day was the first day after creation. Since God finished His work on the seventh day, the eighth day was the beginning of a new order. Here is an interesting sidenote that's worth its weight in gold. Eight souls (Genesis 7:13) were saved from the flood. And what did God do with these eight people after the world was destroyed by water? He began a new order. If this won't make you shout, I'll shout for you.

Not All Living People Are Alive

What? Not all living people are alive! Surely you can't be serious. This sounds like one of the silliest statements ever made by a person who claims to be coherent. How in the world can you say that someone who is living is not alive? I will have to agree that it does sound a little weird. Once you understand that I'm not talking about physical life, things will begin to make sense. The physical body (earth house) was corrupted in Genesis 3 by Adam's disobedience to God's Word, and as long as we live in this earthly realm, we will be living in earth houses (bodies) that continually deteriorate and deteriorate rapidly. With this subtitle, not all living people are alive, I'm distinguishing the difference between the physical and the spiritual. When a person accepts and receives Jesus as their Lord and Savior, God breathes His life into them. They are now spiritually alive even though they still live in bodies that are in the process of decay. Those who have not embraced Christ as their Lord and Savior have physical life, but they are not spiritually alive. They are dead waiting to die (Revelation 20:14–15).

Keep the following statement in mind as you continue reading this section. We are not physical beings who have spirits. We are spiritual beings who live in physical bodies. Our bodies will succumb to death someday, but our spirits will not be affected at all. Once we make the transition out of this world into heaven, we will leave our old bodies behind and be given new glorified bodies that cannot be touched by death or tempted by sin. This is another opportunity to shout and maybe do a little jig.

Let's look at some scriptures that support what you have just read. In Paul's first letter to the church in Corinth, he says, "For the message of the cross is foolishness *to those who are perishing*, but to us who are being saved it is the power of God" (1 Corinthians 1:18 NKJV, emphasis added). Pay close attention to what Paul says about those who have not believed the Gospel and accepted Christ as their Savior. The message of the cross does not appear foolish to them. They are convinced it is foolish. The next thing Paul says about these people without Christ is an eye-opener. He did not say that they were going to perish someday. He said they were already dead. People without Christ may be living, but they are not alive.

Here is some great news. There is no life in death for a child of God. For us death has lost its sting, and the grave no longer has victory over us (1 Corinthians 15:54–55). Death for those who have been born again is exactly the way it was in Genesis 2 before sin entered the human race in Genesis 3. Even though death existed, it had no life. What gave life to death was Adam's sin. He did exactly what God warned him not to do. He ate from the forbidden tree. His sin is what gave life to death, and death killed Adam.

Jesus's victory over death, and the grave is what took life out of death for those who put their trust in Him as their personal Lord and Savior. Death is lifeless to those who have been born from above. At the moment of our born-again experience, God breathed His life into us. Since God's breath is eternal, we will never die! The time will come when we will lay down these old dirt suits we have been assigned and leave this terrestrial realm, but we will never die. He is the life inside of life.

"We know that we have *passed from death to life*, because we love the brethren. He who does not love his brother abides in death" (1 John 3:14 NKJV, emphasis added). Pay close attention to the word order in this verse. John says that as a child of God, we have gone from death to life. I thought the process was from life to death. We live then someday we die. This is true in the natural realm, but it is not in the spiritual realm. Those who are living in the natural state are already considered dead. God has breathed His life into all of His children, making it impossible for them to die. "And you *He made alive, who were dead* in trespasses and sins" (Ephesians 2:1 NKJV, emphasis added). I could give you scripture after scripture that makes this same declaration about being dead (though living) and being made alive. I'll give you a few more verses, and then you can research this for yourself.

"Even though we *were dead* in trespasses, [God] *made us alive* together with Christ (by grace you have been saved)" (Ephesians 2:5 NKJV, emphasis added).

"And you, *being dead* in your trespasses and the uncircumcision of your flesh. *He made us alive* together with Him, having forgiven you all trespasses" (Colossians 2:13 NKJV, emphasis added).

"I tell you the truth, those who listen to my message and believe in God who sent me have eternal life. They will never be condemned for their sins, but *they have already passed from death to life*" (John 5:24 NLT, emphasis added). Once again, the process is from death to life.

We are left with only one conclusion. God is the life in all of life. Without His breath, nothing would exist.

FIFTEEN

The Final Shaking Is Coming

> Then the man of lawlessness will be revealed, but the
> Lord Jesus will slay him with the breath of his mouth
> and destroy him by the splendor of his coming.
> —2 THESSALONIANS 2:8 (NLT)

Here is something that needs to be laid to rest. There is no competition between God and Satan, none. There is only one Creator, and it is not the devil. God created everything with His breath; He sustains everything with His breath, and the time is coming when He destroys our enemies with the same breath. Believe me when I say this, Satan easily recognizes the smell of God's breath, and it makes him very uncomfortable. He has been on the receiving end of the power of God's spoken word. He was blown out of heaven by the breath of his Creator for his attempted coup (Isaiah 14:12–17).

The Sustaining Power of God's Breath

"He [God] existed before anything else, and he holds all creation together" (Colossians 1:17 NLT). If God were to ever withdraw His Word (breath), the natural world would not only come to a screeching halt. It would cease to exist. The only thing that keeps the earthly realm from flying apart is God's breathing. As long as He breathes out, all of creation will be able to breathe in. (Hebrews 11:3). "If God were to take back his spirit and *withdraw his breath*, all life would cease, and humanity would turn again to dust" (Job 34:14–15 NLT, emphasis added). It is high time we get a good grip on what this verse says. When we do, our focus will shift to where it needs to be—on Christ. It will also remind us of our purpose for being in this earthly realm. And that is to share the love of God with the lost and dying before it is eternally too late. Once the final shaking takes place, there will be no hope or second chance given to the people who have rejected God's invitation to life through His Son Jesus Christ.

Who's in Charge

It looks like things are spiraling out of control on this planet we call Earth. All you need to do is watch a few minutes of the evening news to know this is true. It is obvious that a spirit of fear has been released on the human race, and it is driving people to do and say evil things that are sparking more unrest. God told us this day would come through His prophet Isaiah. "Woe to those who *call evil good, and good evil*; Who put darkness for light, and light for darkness; Who put bitter for sweet, and sweet for bitter" (Isaiah 5:20 NKJV, emphasis added). If there is any scripture that describes our day, it is this one.

Since the fall of the human race, evil has always been present. From the time of Genesis 3 to the present, there have been seasons where sin has been rampant, evil has shown its ugly face, the innocent was slaughtered by the millions, corruption inhabited every aspect of society, and immorality was looked upon as being normal. It looked like the coming of Christ would take place at any given moment. The soon return of Jesus Christ has been preached with great passion.

The days in which we live are even more dangerous. Why you may ask? It's because so much time has passed since Christ said He was coming back to this earth to take those who belong to Him home, and it has not happened yet. The passage of time has a tendency to make us forget. Maybe Mr. Winston Churchill was on to something when he said, "Those who fail to learn from history are doomed to repeat it."

The apostle Peter wrote extensively about the days we are living in.

> Beloved, I now write to you this second epistle (in both of which I stir up your pure minds by way of reminder), that you may be mindful of the words which were spoken before by the holy prophets, and of the commandment of us, the apostles of the Lord and Savior, knowing this first: that scoffers will come in the last days, walking according to their own lusts, and saying, "Where is the promise of His coming? For since the fathers fell asleep, all things continue as they were from the beginning of creation." (2 Peter 3:1–4 NKJV, emphasis added)

Scoffers are still around today saying the same thing, "The coming of Christ has been preached for thousands of years, and He hasn't shown up yet. Maybe He's not coming at all."

Let's hear Peter out. "But, beloved, *do not forget this one thing*, that with the Lord one day is as a thousand years, and a thousand years as one day. The Lord is not slack concerning His promise, as some count slackness, *but is longsuffering toward us; not willing that any should perish but that all should come to repentance*" (2 Peter 3:8–9 NKJV, emphasis added). God is not locked into time as you and I are. Let's not forget that He is the one who began time. He was here before the beginning began. Has it ever crossed our mind that God is the one in charge?

Jesus has not returned yet because He is long-suffering toward humanity. He doesn't want one single person to perish. Here is something we need to file away in our memory bank. God has never nor will He ever send anyone to hell. A person chooses to be separated from God for eternity because they chose not to receive His invitation to life. It's time to stop blaming God for sending people to hell.

The history behind Isaiah 6 was a very tumultuous time. Like our day, things were coming apart at the seams. Their greatest need was for strong competent leadership. They had this in King Uzziah, but he had died. It looked like things could not get worse, but they did.

This is when Isaiah had his vision. He saw the Lord. And how was He, Isaiah? "In the year that King Uzziah died, I saw *the Lord sitting on a throne*, high and lifted up, and the train of His robe filled the temple" (Isaiah 6:1 NKJV, emphasis added). The Lord was not walking around wringing His hands wondering what He was going to do. He did not have a council meeting to consider His options on what to do about this situation. Even though man's throne had been momentarily vacated, God was sitting on His. Here's the good news—God is still sitting on His throne. No matter how out of control things may appear, God is still in charge. He has not stopped breathing.

Sometimes it may appear that darkness is dispelling light and evil is conquering good. But that's all it is—an appearance. Once again, the devil has overplayed his hand. God has not abdicated His throne. He is still in control, so we don't need to ask Jesus to take the wheel. We need to buckle our seat belts because we are in for one incredible ride.

When the dark gets darker the light gets brighter

I saw something very interesting several years ago as I was reading through the first five chapters of the book of Genesis—the book of beginnings. I saw something I had never seen before. What came first, night or day? Let's see, "God spoke: 'Light!' And light appeared. God saw that light was good and separated light from dark. God named the light Day, he named the dark Night. It was *evening*, it was *morning*" (Genesis 1:3–5 MSG, emphasis added). The answer to our question is found in the last six words of this passage. The evening was first and then came morning. The order is significant. Because the evening is first, light dispels darkness. If morning had been first, darkness would displace light. I've never ceased to be amazed at how God took care of everything before there was anything. No wonder God says about Himself in Isaiah that there is no one like Him (Isaiah 46:9).

Our purpose for being in this world is to be a light that shines in the darkness, and the darker the night the brighter the light. Jesus talked about this in His sermon on the mountainside. "You are the light of the world. A city that is set on a hill cannot be hidden. Nor do they light a lamp and put it under a basket, but on a lampstand, and it gives light to all who are in the house. Let your light shine before men, that they may see your good works and glorify your Father in heaven" (Matthew 5:14–16 NKJV). We are in a dark, dark season right now. It may appear like darkness has the upper hand, but it hasn't. Darkness must always submit to light. The truth is, darkness is crying out for light and doesn't even know it.

We began this chapter with this statement, there is no competition between God and Satan. Therefore, darkness and light are not opposing forces. Dark is simply the absence of light. When light comes, darkness is no more. I feel a shout coming on. This gives us hope and courage when there is so much despair and fear among believers. Regardless of how bad things may seem or how bad things may get, there's always hope. "Everything was created through him;

nothing—not one thing!—came into being without him. What came into existence was Life, and the Life was Light to live by, The Life–Light blazed out of the darkness; the darkness couldn't put it out" (John 1:3–5 MSG). Here is the bottom line—no matter how dark it may seem we win!

Even in the Dark, You Can Smell the Breath of God

Just because things get hazy or even dark, God is still breathing, He is still sustaining, and He remains faithful. "The faithful love of the Lord never ends! His mercies never cease. Great is his faithfulness; his mercies begin afresh each morning" (Lamentations 3:22–23 NLT, emphasis added). During seasons of darkness, these two verses would be a great place for us to take refuge in. The Lord's love for us never ends. His compassion and faithfulness are not conditional. And his mercies are afresh each morning; and we know what the morning light does, it consumes the darkness. We can always smell the Lord's breath no matter what the conditions may be because His breath is our life.

No matter how challenging times may get we should never give up. We're not in this alone. Our hope is not in this physical world. "That is why we never give up. Though our bodies are dying, our spirits are being renewed every day. For our present troubles are small and won't last very long. Yet they produce for us a glory that vastly outweighs them and will last forever. So we don't look at the troubles we can see now; rather, we fix our gaze on things that cannot be seen. For the things we see now will soon be gone, but the things we cannot see will last forever" (2 Corinthians 4:16–18 NLT). If you find yourself being engulfed by fear and anxiety why not spend some personal time reading and re-reading these three verses until the peace of God consumes you? As we said earlier, there is something more real than what we can see—it is the unseen. What we are able to see will not last forever. What we can't see will never end because it is eternal.

When God Speaks, Things Shake

In 1968 the unit I served with in Vietnam was patrolling an area around the South China Sea. We had made contact with the enemy and we had a pretty good idea they had dug in along the shoreline. There was no way we could get to them without the possibility of receiving a lot of casualties because the terrain was so open. We decided to pull back a little ways and establish a perimeter giving our leadership time to plan a strategy for rooting out the opposing forces.

We were told that there was a battleship anchored several miles offshore and there might be a chance they would help us engage the enemy. We could see the ship on the horizon but it looked like a speck in the middle of all that water. Battleships are equipped with some lethal weaponry that is beyond imagination. If you've ever heard of or seen naval artillery in action, you will never forget it.

Our commanding officer asked for and got permission to have the ship fire a couple of rounds into the area we thought the enemy had bunkered down in. After receiving a grid coordinate the ship fired two rounds at our target. The vessel was so far out at sea that you could actually see the rounds coming our way. It was something to behold. Once the munitions hit the shoreline there was an immediate change in the terrain. I've never heard an explosion like that before or since. I will never forget the unbelievable shaking that the exploding rounds caused. Not only were the bunkers of the enemy completely destroyed, but the collateral damage had taken out well-hidden spider holes used by snipers to carry out stealthy attacks on American soldiers that we knew nothing about.

My experience pales in comparison to what the Israelites heard and felt at Mount Saini exactly two months after they had left Egypt and entered the wilderness of Sinai. The shaking they felt was not caused by artillery rounds; it came from the breath of God. You can be sure of one thing when God speaks, things rattle. And He is not through speaking.

Here's how Moses describes the mountain-shaking moment

when God manifested His presence and power to the Israelites who had been freed from their Egyptian captivity. "On the morning of the third day, *thunder roared and lightning flashed*, and a dense cloud came down on the mountain. There was a long, loud blast from a ram's horn, and *all the people trembled*. Moses led them out from the camp to meet with God and were given specific instructions to remain at the foot of the mountain. All of Mount Sinai was covered with smoke because the Lord had descended on it in the form of fire. The smoke billowed into the sky like smoke from a brick kiln, and *the whole mountain shook violently*" (Exodus 19:16–18 NLT, emphasis added). Sometimes God will speak in a still small voice (1 Kings 19:12), and at other times, He will shake the mountains. I can't imagine what the people were thinking or feeling as the ground underneath their sandals shook violently. Needless to say, God had their attention.

God's Warning of a Final Shaking

The final shaking that God told us is coming will be more devastating than the one in the wilderness of Sinai. This coming shaking will rattle the heavens and earth.

> Be careful that you do not refuse to listen to the One who is speaking. For if the people of Israel did not escape when they refused to listen to Moses, the earthly messenger, we will certainly not escape if we reject the One who speaks to us from heaven! When God spoke from Mount Sinai *his voice shook the earth*, but now he makes another promise: '*Once again I will shake not only the earth but the heavens also*'. This means that all of creation will be shaken and removed so that only unshakable things will remain. Since we are receiving a Kingdom that is

unshakable, let us be thankful and please God by worshipping him with holy fear and awe. For our God is a devouring fire. (Hebrews 12:25–29 NLT, emphasis added)

This end-time event will happen someday because God promised it would, and He always keeps His promises.

There is only one thing that cannot be shaken, and that is the kingdom. If you have accepted and received Jesus Christ as your Lord and Savior, you are a part of this unshakable kingdom. There is nothing that can dislodge us from our union in Christ. This does not mean we will not feel the final shaking, see the shaking, or go through the shaking. All of that depends on a person's eschatological position. Whether we are removed from this planet before, during, or after the tribulation period is debatable. We will leave that argument to those who feel they need to defend their position. But there is one thing we can be certain about, there is coming a final shaking and it will affect everything but the kingdom. Here is a sidenote—the church can be shaken, is being shaken, and will be shaken even more.

Are there any signs we can look for that will alert us that this final season is approaching? Jesus said there is. "When the Son of Man returns, *it will be like it was in Noah's day.* In those days, the people enjoyed banquets and parties and weddings right up to the time Noah entered his boat and the flood came and destroyed them all. And *the world will be as it was in the days of Lot.* People went about their daily business—eating and drinking, buying and selling, farming and building—until the morning Lot left Sodom. Then fire and burning sulfur rained down from heaven and destroyed them all" (Luke 17:26–29 NLT, emphasis added). I realize people have been saying that we are in the end times ever since Jesus ascended into heaven. And it is true that we have been because there has been so much time from Genesis to the present lethargy that has crept in and put the majority of the body of Christ in snooze mode. But to the spiritually sensitive, things are getting clearer and clearer that the time of the final shaking God warned us about is at our front doorsteps. This moment will come suddenly and without warning.

If God's breath has the power to bring things into existence (Genesis 1), His breath is the only thing that has the power to keep everything together, and it is His breath that will bring everything to an end in this earthly realm.

Since we don't know the day or hour this will happen, we need to remain vigilant and prepare for this great exodus. When it happens, there will be no do-overs and no second chances. Where we spend eternity will have been decided. If we listen closely, we may hear Gabriel warming up the Lord's trumpet (1 Thessalonians 4:16). Get ready, get ready.

Listen to what Paul said in his first letter to the church in Thessalonica about the final hour that is coming.

> Now concerning how and when all this will happen, dear brothers and sisters, we don't really need to write you. For you know quite well that the day of *the Lord's return will come unexpectedly, like a thief in the night.* When people are saying, 'Everything is peaceful and secure,' then disaster will fall on them as suddenly as a pregnant woman's labor pains begin. And *there will be no escape.* But you aren't in the dark about these things, dear brothers and sisters, and you won't be surprised when the day of the Lord comes like a thief. For you are all children of the light and of the day; we don't belong to darkness and night. So be on your guard, not asleep like the others. *Stay alert and be clearheaded.* Night is the time when people sleep and drinkers get drunk. But let us who live in the light be clearheaded, protected by the armor of faith and love, and wearing as our helmet the confidence of our salvation. For God

chose to save us through our Lord Jesus Christ, not to pour out his anger on us. Christ died for us so that, whether we are dead or alive when he returns, we can live with him forever. So encourage each other and build each other up, just as you are already doing. (1 Thessalonians 5:1–11 NLT, emphasis added)

The days of Noah and Lot are screaming out a warning to those who will listen. We need to take heed. There are wars and conflicts everywhere, increasing levels of evil abound, wickedness is surging all around the world, and there is an approaching collapse of the global economy. There is social decay, sexual perversion, and more lovers of pleasures rather than lovers of God. This accurately describes the day in which we live.

I minister to a lot of people who don't have confidence that they really have had a born-from-above experience with Christ. They say things like "I prayed the prayer of salvation years ago, but I often have doubts if I was sincere when I prayed. I'm not sure I'm really saved." They will ask me what they should do. I lead them in a prayer right then. But what if they really did get saved when they prayed years earlier? I tell them that I would rather be right twice than wrong once. Remember what I said a moment ago? When the final shaking takes place, there won't be any do-overs. Why would you want to run the risk of not having confidence in your salvation? This would be a good time to bow your head and pray a prayer like this, Father, I am doing what you told me to do to be saved, and I believe you will do what you said you would do—save me. I ask for forgiveness of my sins. I believe Jesus took my place on the cross, died my death, and arose on the third day. I accept and receive Jesus Christ as my Lord and Savior. I exchange my old nature for a new one. I thank you for hearing my prayer and for saving my soul. I am now a part of your kingdom.

We began this chapter with 2 Thessalonians 2:8. I think it would be appropriate to end with it as well. "Then the man of lawlessness [the antichrist] will be revealed, but *the Lord Jesus will kill him with the breath of his mouth* and destroy him by the splendor of his coming" (2 Thessalonians 2:8 NLT, emphasis added). Let's live as if Christ died yesterday, arose today, and is coming back tomorrow. We win.

EPILOGUE

With the arrival of Jesus, the Messiah, that fateful dilemma is
resolved. Those who enter into Christ's being-here-for-us no
longer have to live under a continuous, low-lying black cloud.
A new power is in operation. The Spirit of life in Christ, like a
strong wind, has magnificently cleared the air, freeing you from a
fated lifetime of brutal tyranny at the hands of sin and death.
—ROMANS 8:1–2 (MSG)

The breath of God is like a strong wind that has freed us from sin's
captivity. This is the declaration of these two verses found in Romans
8. God's breath has not only set us free from sin's dominion, but His
breath keeps us free. We are not just free we are truly free. "So if the
Son sets you free, you are truly free" (John 8:36 NLT).

Every breath we take is a miracle because we are breathing in
the life of God. If you find this hard to believe, then ask yourself
this question, why do we gasp and struggle so hard when we get the
wind knocked out of us? Our bodies cannot survive without air in
our lungs. Without oxygen, we won't be in this earthly realm for
very long. And the breath we carry inside our lungs has been given
to us by our Creator as a gift. He is the air we breathe. He is the life
inside of life.

I was blown away the first time I heard Amy Grant sing "Breath
of Heaven" (released in 1992). It is also called "Mary's Song." It
addresses the miracle of God using Mary's womb as His chosen
vehicle to bring Himself into this world in the person of Jesus. This

is absolutely mind-blowing: Mary carried the breath of heaven in her womb. God is the life inside of life. Let me add to what I just said. Mary actually carried God inside her twice. The first time she carried God in her womb in the person of Jesus. The second time she carried God in her heart in the person of the Holy Spirit.

This is impossible for the human mind to grasp. I can't imagine how Mary must have felt when she heard the message that was sent to her from the throne of God about being handpicked to give birth to Jesus, the Son of God. How does the human brain comprehend something like this? It can't because this was a miracle, and miracles are incomprehensible. Maybe this is why Mary had a difficult time trying to explain her condition to Joseph, and he had a hard time understanding what she was telling him about her encounter with the angel Gabriel. It is impossible to understand or explain a miracle. Maybe this is why it is called a miracle.

Mary had never been with a man, so her question to the angel Gabriel was understandable, "How can this happen." "The angel answered, 'the Holy Spirit will come upon you, the power of the Highest hover over you; Therefore, the child you bring to birth will be called Holy, Son of God'" (Luke 1:35 MSG). Just like the breath of God hovered (brooding) over the earth in the creation account found in the book of Genesis, the breath (spirit) of God would breathe His life into Mary's womb.

We Carry the Life of God in Us

"The earth was without form, and void; and darkness was on the face of the deep. And the Spirit of God was hovering [brooding, breathing] over the face of the waters" (Genesis 1:2 NKJV, emphasis added). Time in this earthly realm was about to begin, and it would begin with God breathing out so all of creation could breathe in. The power of God's breath brought all of creation into existence and order, and it is His breath that keeps everything He created intact.

This is why I say that God is the life inside of life. This same life-giving breath would hover over Mary. She would carry God's life inside of her life.

"I will not leave you orphaned. I'm coming back. In just a little while the world will no longer see me, but you're going to see me because *I am alive and you're about to come alive*. At that moment you will know absolutely that *I'm in my Father*, and *you're in me*, and *I'm in you*" (John 14:18–20 MSG, emphasis added). Can you think of anything that can compare with having the Creator of all things, the sustainer of the universe and beyond, the one who has no beginning or end, and the giver of all life living inside of you? As a child of God, this is exactly what we're carrying around twenty-four seven—the life of God. If we ever get a hold of this truth, life for us would be forever changed. I'm not talking about having this truth in our heads and being able to quote the verses. I'm talking about the kind of life we would live knowing that God is living His life through us. The new creation we have been made in Christ is alive and will never die. "And whoever lives and believes in Me *shall never die*. Do you believe this" (John 11:26 NKJV, emphasis added)? A good question is do you believe this? Only you have the answer.

As Mary carried Jesus in her physical womb, we carry the life of God in our spiritual wombs. This is the theme of chapter 14 of this book *When God Breathes*. God is the life inside of life. Without Him, we are living but not alive. When we embrace Him as our Lord and Savior, we move from death to life. "But God, who is rich in mercy, because of his great love with which he loved us, even *when we were dead* in trespasses *made us alive* together with Christ (by grace you have been saved) and raised us up together in the heavenly places in Christ Jesus" (Ephesians 2:4–6 NKJV, emphasis added).

"*Everything* of God gets expressed in him, so *you can see and hear him clearly*. You don't need a telescope, a microscope, or a horoscope to realize the fullness of Christ, and the emptiness of the universe without him. *When you come to him, that fullness comes together for you, too*. His power extends over everything" (Colossians 2:9–10

MSG, emphasis added). When we accepted and received Christ as our Lord and Savior, we did not get His life on an installment plan, a little today, more tomorrow; it is if we work hard enough and don't stump our toes. When God took up residence within us in the person of the Holy Spirit, we got all of Him. We are not His spiritual Airbnb. We are the temple of the Holy Spirit. Our Creator owns all of us. Listen to what Paul said to the Christians who lived in Corinth about this. "Or didn't you realize that *your body is a sacred place, the place of the Holy Spirit*? Don't you see that you can't live however you please, squandering what God paid such a high price for? *The physical part of you is not some piece of property belonging to the spiritual part of you. God owns the whole works.* So let people see God in and through your body" (1 Corinthians 6:19–20 MSG, emphasis added). When God moved into your life, He became a permanent resident. Never forget that God owns the house (your life). He paid for it with His life.

The way God gave life to the first Adam was by breathing His spirit into him. The source of life has not changed. Only God can give life. When a person repents and receives Christ as their personal Lord and Savior, the Holy Spirit imparts life to this person by breathing the life of God into them. God formed a man from the dust of the ground and then breathed into him the breath of life (Genesis 2:7). When this happened, the man (Adam) became a living being, a living soul, and a speaking spirit. The Holy Spirit imparts life the same way to those who surrender their lives to Christ. He breathes the breath of life into them. He becomes the life inside of their lives.

God's Intent from the Beginning of Time

The epitaph on the tombstone of many believers could read something like this, "Here lies a person who never enjoyed their new-creation life." This is sad but true. The majority of Christians have no clue about their new-creation identities. I am convinced that it is not because they don't want to know, they have never been taught. But the truth is you can't teach something you don't know. This is why most believers are working hard trying to become what Christ has already made them to be.

What difference would it make in the way we live every day if we knew and were convinced that God, in the person of the Holy Spirit, is living on the inside of us? I have the answer to this question—peace and rest. This was God's intent from the very beginning of time. We are told in Genesis 1 that God finished His work (breathing creation into existence) on the sixth day. On the seventh day, God rested from His work. Humanity's first day was God's rest day. Are you beginning to see the picture? Humanity began with life with God after all the work had been done. The same is true for believers. Christ did all the work so we could enjoy life with Him in peace and rest. We don't have to do things for God to be accepted by Him. We get to do things for Him because we are accepted by Him, apart from works.

As children of God, we have something in common with Mary. God has chosen us as His permanent residence. He lives inside us in the person of the Holy Spirit. God is breathing His life in and through us. As long as He breathes out, we will breathe in. It's time for every believer to take a deep breath, relax, and breathe slowly.

"God has transmitted his very substance into every Scripture, for it is God-breathed. It will empower you by its instruction and correction, giving you the strength to take the right direction and lead you deeper into the path of godliness"* (2 Timothy 3:16 TPT, emphasis added).

Printed in the United States
by Baker & Taylor Publisher Services

Printed in the United States
by Baker & Taylor Publisher Services